The Human Relations Experience

Exercises in Multicultural Nonsexist Education

The Human Relations Experience

Exercises in Multicultural Nonsexist Education

Nicholas Colangelo
The University of Iowa

Dick Dustin
The University of Iowa

Cecelia H. Foxley
Utah State University

Brooks/Cole Publishing Company
Monterey, California

Brooks/Cole Publishing Company
A Division of Wadsworth, Inc.

Printed in the United States of America
10 9 8 7 6 5 4 3 2 1

Library of Congress Cataloging in Publication Data

Colangelo, Nicholas.
The human relations experience.

Bibliography: p.
1. Interpersonal relations--Study and
teaching. 2. Sexism. 3. Racism. 4. Educational sociology. I. Dustin, Dick, date
II. Foxley, Cecelia H. III. Title.
HM132.C55   302   81-18104
ISBN 0-534-01104-7   AACR2

Subject Editor: Claire Verduin
Manuscript Editor: William Waller
Production Editor: Suzanne Ewing
Interior and Cover Design: Katherine Minerva

Preface

One of the most significant trends in education today is the emphasis on human relations training. Unfortunately, most books and workbooks on human relations have dealt with a specific topic such as communication skills, racism, sexism, or the nature of prejudice. This workbook is unique in dealing with all these critical issues. We believe that these issues are related--that we cannot talk about racism, for example, without recognizing its similarities to sexism. Racism and sexism are more comprehensible when viewed as part of the phenomena of prejudice and stereotyping. And, learning about racism and sexism is inadequate unless we have the skills to communicate in new ways with people of a different culture or gender.

This workbook has been designed to provide learning experiences in the integration of communication skills with the issues of race, sex, and prejudice. It is divided into five chapters.

Chapter 1 presents a rationale for human relations education as well as guidelines for using the workbook. It has been our experience that most workbooks in this field offer a potpourri of exercises. This workbook, in contrast, is organized around our model of human relations education. Instructors and students will be able to relate the workbook exercises to our conceptualization, providing an integration of practice and theory.

Chapter 2 deals with practicing and applying human relations skills. These communication skills are the foundations for all the other exercises.

Chapter 3 provides exercises related to sexism. It includes activities designed to increase awareness of one's own attitudes and behaviors as well as of the many sexist elements in the schools.

Chapter 4 includes exercises and activities designed to increase awareness about various cultural groups. In addition, students are required to examine their own attitudes about race and culture.

Chapter 5 deals with the nature of prejudice and stereotyping in various facets of society. Students can examine their attitudes regarding the handicapped, homosexuals, the aged, and other groups that have typically been victims of prejudice.

We have also included a glossary and a resource section listing further materials on human relations.

The exercises and activities in this workbook will require the personal involvement of both students and instructors. We don't believe that any of us can sincerely examine our attitudes and values in the "abstract." In addition to this personal involvement, instructors should provide a content base for the various chapters through assigned readings and lectures. If instructors can assign stimulating and relevant articles, these can add to the "personal" contribution that each student will provide. One book of readings that complements this workbook is <u>Multicultural Nonsexist Education: A Human Relations Approach</u> edited by Colangelo, N., Foxley, C. H., & Dustin, D. (Kendall/Hunt Publishers, 1940 Kerper Boulevard, Dubuque, Iowa).

A SPECIAL NOTE TO INSTRUCTORS ON USING THIS WORKBOOK

This workbook has been designed to be comprehensive and flexible. However, its effectiveness is also dependent on how each instructor adapts it to his or her needs. Three points may help you use this material.

A. Chapter 2, "Practicing and Applying Human Relations Skills," is a necessary component for all the other chapters. Students are required in Chapter 2 to practice and learn effective means of communication. Without these essential tools, changing stereotypes about race, sex, and other issues will be difficult. We feel it is imperative that the skills learned in Chapter 2 be applied as students progress through this workbook. The exercises in Chapters 3, 4, and 5 assume the application of effective communication skills. It is important that the instructor remind students of the skills learned in Chapter 2 and, when appropriate, *explicitly* refer to these skills when doing exercises in the remainder of this workbook.

B. The exercises in this workbook have been organized sequentially, so that each exercise builds on information and experience from previous ones. While we have attempted to include a variety of exercises, the instructor needs to choose those that best fit his or her goals for the class or workshop. It is not our expectation that students need to do every exercise to benefit from this workbook. Nor do we expect that an equal amount of time be spent on each section. On the one hand, if students are relatively well experienced and knowledgeable in communication skills, we would recommend that minimal time be spent on Chapter 2. On the other hand, a particular class may have difficulties in dealing with issues related to sexism and nonsexist education. In this case an instructor may want to spend a longer time on the exercises and discussions provided in Chapter 3.

C. While it has been our intention to make this workbook as comprehensive as possible, it is impossible for us to have an exercise for each identifiable cultural group or issue. Instead, we have tried to design our exercises so that they can be easily adapted to specific cultural groups or issues. We believe students learn better when they can deal with issues that are immediate to their daily lives. We encourage instructors to substitute specific cultural groups or issues that are important to their geographical area into these exercises. With minimal changes the exercises offer a format that is adaptable to individual needs.

We believe that human relations education is an extremely challenging topic as well as one central to the well-being of society. We hope this workbook will stimulate vibrant, thoughtful human interaction.

We wish to thank our colleagues Debbie Floyd, Al Hood, and Ralph Roberts for field-testing some of the exercises included in this workbook. We also thank Donald R. Atkinson, Donald Helberg, and William R. Martin for their reviews of the workbook. Finally, we thank Reta Litton, Ginny Volk, and Carrie Kurtz, our typists, and Bill Waller and Sue Ewing for their editorial assistance.

Nicholas Colangelo
Dick Dustin
Cecelia H. Foxley

Contents

3 Recognizing and Changing Sexist Attitudes and Behaviors 83

4 Recognizing and Diminishing Cultural and Racial Biases 129

5   Recognizing and Dealing with Other Kinds of Prejudices and Stereotypes   173

A   Appendix: Glossary   215

B   Appendix: Resources   219

The Human Relations Experience

Exercises in Multicultural Nonsexist Education

1
A Framework for
Using the Workbook

Among the most visible and progressive legislative changes in U.S. education have been those protecting the rights of groups of people in our society. Examples of such legislation include Title IX of the Education Amendments of 1972, which prohibits discrimination on the basis of sex; Section 503 of the Rehabilitation Act of 1973; and the Education for All Handicapped Children Act of 1975 (Public Law 94-142), which assures the handicapped a free public education. Along with these federal mandates, some states are requiring human relations education for teacher certification. Such requirements include not only basic skills in effective communication but also the understanding of and ability to relate to individuals from various subgroups. These requirements are aimed at prejudices and stereotypes that result in racism, sexism, discrimination against the handicapped, and other dehumanizing biases. The term *human relations* is used in this workbook in this broad, complete sense.[1]

EXPERIENTIAL LEARNING

This workbook is designed to help teachers and teachers-in-training sharpen and refine their human relations abilities. It is based on the premise that we learn more effectively by doing, by experiencing. This premise is particularly appropriate when dealing with a comprehensive concept of human relations education. To expect people to learn to communicate and relate effectively with others by merely reading a book or listening to a lecture on communication skills is unrealistic. The reading and listening are only part of the learning. What completes the learning cycle and makes the content meaningful is experiencing and applying what has been read and heard. Thus, our idea of learning combines cognitive learning and experiential learning.

This workbook is not intended to take the place of theoretical and conceptual readings in human relations. Rather, it is designed to be

---

[1]Parts of this chapter have been adapted from N. Colangelo, C. H. Foxley, and D. Dustin (Eds.). Multicultural Nonsexist Education: A Human Relations Approach. Dubuque, Iowa: Kendall/Hunt, © 1979.

used in tandem with such readings. As we have said, it is experiential and applied learning that individualizes and gives personal
meaning and relevance to concepts and ideas.

COMPREHENSIVE APPROACH TO HUMAN RELATIONS EDUCATION

In addition to these two types of learnings, our definition of a
comprehensive human relations education gives a central place to
interpersonal relations and communications training (usually termed
human relations training). Finally, it also includes three categories
of subject matter: nonsexist education, multicultural education, and
special issues dealing with prejudice, stereotyping, and bias. With
desegregation, nonsexist education, and mainstreaming playing an
increasingly important part in education, it is highly unlikely that
a teacher will have only students of his or her own culture and
background. Our comprehensive concept is also a reflection of the
need for teachers to comply with federal regulations requiring the

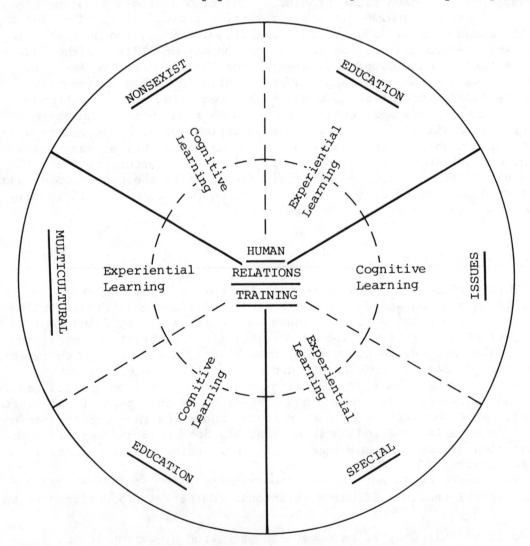

*FIGURE 1-1. Conceptualization of a Comprehensive Approach to
Human Relations Education*

protection of student rights and prohibiting unfair treatment and discrimination.

Human relations training (communication skills) is the common denominator for the other areas of our comprehensive model. It is the core of human relations education. Figure 1-1 illustrates our conceptualization of this comprehensive approach. Each of the major components in the figure will now be discussed and related to the appropriate chapter in the workbook.

HUMAN RELATIONS TRAINING

Human relations training encompasses a recognition of the *humanness* of people. The basic tenet is that all people have a common bond by the mere fact that they are human. Humanness denotes the *commonality* of people as well as their *individuality*. It is commonality that provides the basis for people to understand and respect one another. Individuality provides the basis for people to value and allow for differences.

Human relations training also encompasses *interaction* between two or more individuals. This human interaction is an interchange of each person's commonality and individuality. In human interaction each person's commonality and individuality can be viewed as *attributes* and *skills*. Attributes include values, feelings, beliefs, and attitudes. Skills include self-awareness, listening, genuineness, concreteness, self-disclosure, and confrontation.

The authors of this workbook see skills as an important part, but certainly not the whole. At the same time, focusing on single elements of human interaction, or skills, allows them to be defined, observed, and practiced. Finally, with feedback and encouragement, individuals can incorporate single skills into a personal style. In this workbook, training in human relations skills is viewed as a means toward effective humanizing of both practicing and prospective teachers.

Chapter 2, "Practicing and Applying Human Relations Skills," provides exercises and experiences designed to help you understand your own attitudes, values, and communication skills as well as those of the people with whom you interact. The experiential learning exercises are arranged in such a way as to enable you to build on your new insights in order to acquire further learning.

NONSEXIST EDUCATION

Nonsexist education is free of stereotypic elements. It encourages the development of the full range of skills, knowledge, and interests of both male and female students. The attitudes and behaviors of teachers and other school personnel are unbiased. Students are assisted in exploring nontraditional interests and subjects. They are encouraged to develop according to their own interests and abilities without being concerned about the "appropriateness" for their sex. Nontraditional role models are provided within the school system itself, and examples are brought in from the community, such as a female doctor and a male nurse. School policies do not treat male and female students differently. All courses, educational programs, and extracurricular programs are open to members of both sexes. Stereotypic and sexist elements in instructional materials are pointed out to students and replaced by unbiased materials as soon as possible. In short, nonsexist education does not limit the development and learning of either male or female students on the basis of their sex.

Human relations training helps men and women understand the detrimental effects of sexism and work together in broadening and changing traditional sex roles. Sex-role studies--the examination of the development of sex roles and accompanying socialization processes--help men and women better understand the impact of socialization and sex typing on their own lives. By merging human relations training and sex-role studies, members of both sexes can explore new, expanded sex roles and take advantage of a greater range of opportunities and life-styles.

One of the main objectives of nonsexist educational programs is eliminating sex-role prejudice and stereotyping. With that accomplished, the goal of equality of educational opportunity for the sexes can be reached.

Chapter 3, "Recognizing and Changing Sexist Attitudes," presents exercises and activities designed to increase self-awareness of sexist thinking and behavior as well as an awareness of the many sexist elements in the schools. Also included are activities for promoting change in the classroom and the entire school system.

MULTICULTURAL EDUCATION

An effective multicultural-education program needs two components: human relations training and ethnic studies. We have already discussed human relations training as learning to relate on the "human" level. However, we believe that simply to relate to people because they are human misses some specific appreciation of their uniqueness that can enrich communication and understanding. The richness and uniqueness of people can be attributed in part to their ethnic (this includes cultural and racial) background. While we are all humans, we belong to specific groups. To fully understand people we need to understand their cultural group as well.

Our critique of many programs labeled "multicultural" is that they are merely ethnic studies programs, since they do not include human relations training. To combat racial prejudice and stereotyping, people need the skills and experience to communicate effectively, which can be learned through human relations training. They also need knowledge and awareness of the uniqueness of cultural groups, which can be learned through ethnic studies. A multicultural program that includes only one of these areas is minimally effective at best.

Chapter 4, "Recognizing and Combatting Cultural and Racial Biases," includes experiential learning activities designed to increase participants' awareness about various cultural groups.

A comprehensive approach to human relations education recognizes the tremendous variation within groups of people--the concept of individuality carried to its fullest. Sexism and racism are only two of many types of prejudice. People experience prejudice and stereotyping because of age, physical and mental disabilities, giftedness, sexual preferences, obesity, baldness--the list goes on and on. But whatever the type of prejudice and stereotyping, it can be combatted through human relations education that combines training in interpersonal skills with knowledge and awareness of the particular type of prejudice. Figure 1-2 is another way of illustrating our conceptualization of a comprehensive approach to human relations education.

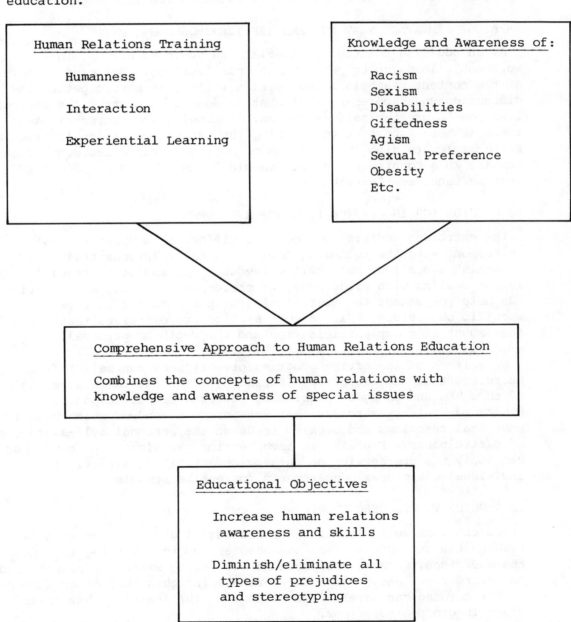

FIGURE 1-2. A Comprehensive Approach to Human Relations Education

Chapter 5, "Recognizing and Dealing with Other Kinds of Prejudices and Stereotypes," identifies some of these special issues and provides exercises and activities designed to help you recognize a variety of prejudices and stereotypes. It also presents several exercises of a very general nature that can be readily applied to any population or issue.

USES OF THIS WORKBOOK

This workbook is designed as a practical tool to help teachers, in-service leaders, and individuals who wish to further their own awareness of human relations issues and concepts. Three of the specific uses for which the book is intended are discussed below.

AS A SUPPLEMENTARY TEXT FOR PRE-SERVICE PROGRAMS

As an addition to reading materials in human relations, this workbook allows you to personalize your learning. Selected aspects of the content reach into your personal life, as participation and discussion underscores part of what is done in a class. The exercises lead you to greater self-awareness. Expanding your personal experience is more important to learning than simple cognitive information. For example, reading about sexism or multicultural classrooms often results in a cognitive list of "shoulds" and "should nots" rather than personalized learning.

AS A GUIDE FOR IN-SERVICE PROGRAMS AND WORKSHOPS

The exercises in this workbook are divided into chapters that correspond with the following topics: human relations training, nonsexist education, multicultural education, and other special issues dealing with prejudices and stereotyping. This organization can help you select the most meaningful portions for your own specific objectives. Within each section are exercises that vary the amount of group participation and the depth of personal exploration.

Organizers of in-service programs or workshops can select from exercises that feature group discussion, fostering the sharpening of thoughts and changes in thinking patterns of participants. Others may select exercises that are more open-ended, which highlight emotional reactions and seek to focus on the personal self-awareness of participants. Finally, in each section exercises are found that can apply the pre-service or in-service activities directly to individual classrooms, departments, or entire schools.

AS A GUIDE TO PERSONAL GROWTH

You can take yourself through a meaningful growth experience by reading the introduction in each chapter and then working through the exercises. Spaces are provided for you to write out answers and to record reactions. Often the personal insights that occur through such recording can have as much impact as the learning that takes place in group discussions.

2
Practicing and Applying Human Relations Skills

INTRODUCTION

Every teacher is aware of the importance of communication in the classroom. Much of the success or failure of learning revolves around the everyday communication between teacher and student. The following examples may sound familiar.

"Can't you follow directions?"
"I don't remember what you said."
"I didn't hear you."
"I didn't mean for you to read those pages."

Each human relations skill taken up in this chapter can be defined and practiced in the classroom (George & Glazer-Waldman, 1979). Together, these single skills combine into the rich, varied complexity of communication. The human relations skills described in this chapter are:

1. careful attending
2. open questions
3. responding to content
4. responding to feelings
5. genuineness and self-disclosure
6. feedback
7. confrontation

DEFINITIONS

As pointed out in Chapter 1, human relations skills are the core components for increasing understanding and reducing bias among groups and individuals. Understanding and mastering the few skills in this chapter can result in improved communication. For each of the skills, a brief definition is followed by the purpose of the skill and a few examples. This section is intended to serve as a basis for the exercises that follow. More complete descriptions of the skills can be found elsewhere (Carkhuff, 1969; Dustin & George, 1977; Egan, 1975, 1977; Gazda, et al., 1977; Ivey, 1971).

CAREFUL ATTENDING

Careful attending can be defined as concentrating on the meaning of a message while indicating interest. A teacher who is attending carefully to a student will listen for more than the words. This skill is mostly nonverbal but also includes some verbal responses. The behaviors involved in careful attending include:

Facing or looking at the speaker.
Looking at the expression and posture of the speaker.
Facial expressions that reflect the speaker's meaning (smiles for pleasant messages, serious expressions for some, and so on).
Communicating phrases when appropriate, such as "Wow!" "Really?"
Putting down distracting materials while listening.

Students can begin using the careful attending skill early in training because it is basic and serves as a foundation for skills that follow.

The purposes of careful attending include increasing the understanding of the listener and communicating to the speaker that the listener believes that what is being said is important. Two examples of careful attending follow.

Example A: Student, looking troubled, says "I don't know if I should bother you."
Teacher, sitting at desk, puts down book, looks at student, and says "Sure."

Example B: Teacher A, looking glum, says "What a rotten day."
Teacher B, who is hurrying down the hall, stops, turns toward teacher A, and says "Oh?"

OPEN AND CLOSED QUESTIONS

Open questions are those that require more than a yes or no response. These questions are an invitation to explore the person's thinking and feelings. Teachers are all too familiar with answers such as "I don't know," "Yes," and "No." One way to encourage students to elaborate is to phrase open questions, not closed ones. One hint on how to ask open questions: begin them with words such as *how*, *when*, *what*, or *where*.

The purpose of open questions is to encourage the speaker to elaborate on the message rather than just providing a one-word answer. Two examples of closed and open questions follow.

	Closed Questions	Open Questions
Example A:	"Do you like school?"	"How are things going in school?"
Example B:	"Do you like your teacher?"	"What do you like about your teacher?"

RESPONDING TO CONTENT

Two skills are included in responding to content: restating and paraphrasing. Restating is essentially a word-for-word repetition of the content of the speaker. Its usefulness is found in such specific situations as receiving directions or mediating conflict between angry students. Whenever exact understanding is important, restating is useful.

Paraphrasing is used more frequently than restating. A paraphrase is a shortened version of the message that changes some of the words but retains the meaning.

Some hints for effective restating and paraphrasing are:

Start responses with "You"--for example, "You say that . . ."
Listen carefully to the "essence" of the speaker.
Try to be brief.
Avoid adding your own judgments.

The purpose of restating is to determine the accuracy of a listener's understanding of a message. Restatements allow both the speaker and listener to be sure that their communication has been effective. The purpose of a paraphrase is to communicate what has been heard. The paraphraser shows interest and a desire to understand the speaker. Both these skills serve to minimize confusion in communication.

Example A (Restating):   "I can't get this assignment."
                         "You can't get it, eh?"
Example B (Paraphrasing): "I have to watch my baby brother, do
                          yard work, and clean my room. My parents
                          are on me all the time."
                          "So you've got lots of jobs and your
                          parents are on you."

RESPONDING TO FEELINGS

Reflecting feelings is a skill in which the listener repeats the message in a way that highlights the speaker's feelings. This is done by stating a feeling word in the response. Two examples follow:

Example A: Student: "Boy, things are going well. I've got all
            my assignments in. I feel great."
            Teacher: "It feels good to be all caught up."
Example B: Student: "Everybody has a date for the prom but me.
            I feel left out."
            Teacher: "You're really feeling down about no date for
            the prom."

The purpose of a reflection of feeling is to personalize the communication. The most personal aspect of listening is to show that not only the message but also how the speaker feels about the message is being understood. Some hints that make reflecting feelings effective are:

Use a feeling word to highlight the speaker's message.
Avoid adding your own judgments or feelings.
Focus on the speaker rather than the content of the speaker's story.
Be brief.

Responding may also include more than reflecting a feeling a speaker expresses. Sometimes subtle or verbally unexpressed feelings are embedded in a message. Responding to such feelings can be difficult. The purpose of such responses is to show others that you are interested in their feelings and that you are sensitive to them. Here are some behavioral hints for responding to subtle feelings:

Ask about the feelings.
Use a feeling word to highlight the subtle message.
Avoid sounding judgmental about the subtle feelings.
Attend to nonverbal expressions to verify your perception of the
   feeling.

Example A: Student: "I have to watch my baby brother, do yard
                     work, and clean my room. They're on me all the time."
           Teacher: "You must be feeling overwhelmed."
Example B: Student: "I've applied for a scholarship. I don't
                     know what chance I really have of getting it."
           Teacher: "You seem uncertain about your chances of
                     getting the scholarship."

GENUINENESS AND SELF-DISCLOSURE

Self-disclosure is the communication of one's opinions, thoughts,
values, and the like. Genuineness is a specific form of self-disclosure, involving communicating the speaker's specific feelings in a
concrete fashion in which the nonverbal expressions and the declared
feelings of the speaker are congruent.

Example A (self-disclosure): "I think this room needs a coat of
                               paint."
Example B (genuineness): "I get depressed whenever I'm in this
                          room."

Genuineness and self-disclosure can be made effective by applying
the following behavioral hints:

State feelings specifically.
Start statements with "I."
Keep statements concise.
Relate personal experiences to the listener(s).
Check out whether the listener understood the point.

The purpose of these two skills includes opening up communication
to a two-way exchange in which the student finds out more about the
teacher. Genuineness communicates how the teacher is feeling. Self-
disclosure helps the student get to know something of the teacher's
past, opinions, and values. The purpose is to build trust and to
increase the depth of communication.

FEEDBACK

Feedback is the skill of describing behaviors and, at times, giving
reactions to them. The purpose of feedback is to try to influence the
receiver's behavior. "I like the way you spoke up in the meeting
yesterday" is an example of giving feedback in the hopes that the
person will repeat the behavior. Another important purpose of feedback is to increase the receiver's self-understanding. "I notice you
fidget with your hands quite a bit when it's your turn to talk" is an
example of feedback that would add to the receiver's awareness.
Effective feedback is a powerful learning tool.
Behavioral hints for making feedback effective are:

Describe behaviors as much as possible.
Avoid global labels or judgments.

Limit feedback to your own observations. (Repeating what "they" are saying is not usually very effective.)
Limit feedback to one aspect of a person's behavior at a time.

Two examples of feedback follow:

	Ineffective	Effective
Example A:	"You're always late!"	"I notice you're coming late to class almost every day. That really bothers me."
Example B:	"You never want to talk about Fred."	"I notice that when we discuss Fred you change the subject. That makes me think you'd rather not talk about your relationship with him."

CONFRONTATION

Confrontation has usually been described as a skill of communication in typical human relations training courses. We believe that this is not a helpful description of confrontation and does not approximate the way most people understand it.

We find it most useful to conceptualize confrontation as the use of communication skills in a confrontational situation which has some unique attributes that distinguish it from other types of situations. When we speak of confrontation in human relations training we are referring to a situation that typically contains the following attributes:

The issue has meaning or is of importance. (Differences over superficial or inconsequential issues to the involved parties are not confrontive situations.)
The issue has a high emotional investment for the people involved.
The outcome can have a strong negative or positive effect on those involved.
The issue is forced to the forefront. Those involved must either deal with it openly or knowingly not deal with it.
The use of communication skills is required to a high degree.

Thus, we conceptualize confrontation as an integrative skill that requires using all the other skills discussed. It can be either effective or ineffective depending on the level of communication skills involved. Confrontational situations in which people use communication skills to a high degree yield resolution based on understanding. Confrontational situations in which people do not use communication skills to a high degree lead to misunderstanding and unresolved issues. Figure 2-1 illustrates our conceptualization of confrontation.

Here is an example of effective and ineffective confrontation. One person (White) confronts another person (Black) about the Black's attitudes. Assume that both find the issue meaningful.

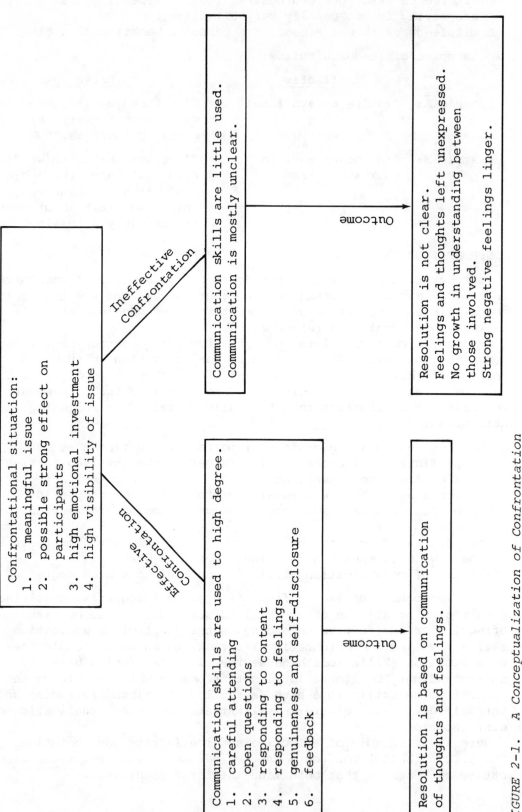

FIGURE 2-1. *A Conceptualization of Confrontation*

Confronter (White) - W
Confrontee (Black) - B

W: I'm fed up with your attitude about Whites.
B: What are you talking about?
W: Don't play games--your attitudes are obvious to everyone.
B: How do you know what's going on in my head?
W: I've got eyes and ears, don't I?
B: Be specific--give me a "for instance."
W: There's so many I can't think of just one. And besides, I'm so fed up with your games I don't think it's worth my time to talk about it.
B: That's cool--if you haven't got the time, then I haven't got the time.
W: This is stupid--let's get on to something else.

Note: From the above interaction it is obvious that there are strong feelings involved and, while there was a confrontational situation, the communication skills used were so minimal that no progress was made. An issue has been raised, but it has been left with confusion and perhaps negative feelings.

Confronter (White) - W
Confrontee (Black) - B

W: I'm bothered with some of the things you say about Whites and some of your nonverbal behaviors when the class talks about White-Black issues.
B: What are you talking about?
W: One instance was yesterday when you said "All Whites are basically racist." That bothered me, because I felt you were lumping me in this category of "all Whites." I felt you didn't know how I felt about race issues, yet you assumed I was a racist because I'm White. When you say things like that I have two reactions. One is anger at you because you're accusing me of something you assume to be true. The other feeling is frustration-- frustration that somehow you've made up your mind about me and you probably won't listen to what I have to say.
B: Hmm--OK. I see what you're saying and I do remember making that statement yesterday. I guess even nonverbally I made faces to let my feelings be known. The thing is, I believe that about Whites.
W: Well, why don't you ask me about how I see things. I could listen and try to understand where you are coming from a lot more if I felt you were listening to me as an individual and not as a representative of some group.

Note: The confrontational situation is only beginning, but it is clear that it is headed in a very different direction from the dialogue illustrating ineffective confrontation. There are several elements in this confrontation that make it potentially effective.

W does not simply state a feeling (I'm fed up!) but specifically points to behaviors and incidences that bother him. When B asks for clarification, W is specific. It is not B who is attacked but some of his behaviors. W not only specifies the bothersome behaviors but also lets B know how they affect him ("I feel angry and frustrated"). In addition, W has made an offer to conduct a dialogue, indicating that he wants to understand as well as be understood. Though we don't know where this dialogue will lead, the elements of effective communication are present, making it possible for both W and B to express their thoughts and feelings in a clear and honest way to each other.

GOALS OF THIS CHAPTER

Figure 2-2 summarizes the human relations skills covered in the exercises that follow. The exercises and activities of this chapter are designed to help you familiarize yourself with your current human relations skills and help you develop more effective interactions. The exercises let you practice and improve your communication skills within as well as outside the classroom.

The exercises are designed to help you to explore your communication patterns and receive feedback from others. Reading about communication does not necessarily lead to more effective classroom behaviors. Through participation in small groups, pairing with partners, and structured feedback sessions, you can evaluate your own behaviors.

In addition, group-discussion questions about each skill are provided, so that you can listen to and think about others' reactions to your skills. Since some of the material of this chapter is very personal, it is essential that you share reactions to the exercises. You have been communicating for years and have developed your "way of talking." To change these communication patterns may be seen as threatening. However, to improve human relations in the classroom you need to see the value of a particular skill, learn to perform it, and apply it in the classroom in your own personal style.

REFERENCES

Carkhuff, R. R. Helping and human relations. Vols. 1 & 2. New York: Holt, Rinehart & Winston, 1969.

Dustin, R., & George, R. Action counseling for behavior change. Cranston, R. I.: Carroll Press, 1977.

Skill	Communication Elements		What Message the Skill Conveys	Effect on Communication
	Verbal	Non-Verbal		
1. Careful Attending	+	++	Listener is interested in the speaker. Listener wants to hear more.	Promotes trust. Encourages the speaker to communicate further.
2. Open Questions	+		Listener desires to hear more from speaker. Listener is interested.	Enhances elaboration of thoughts and feelings. Increases two-way communication.
3. Responding to Content (Restating) (Paraphrasing)	+ +		Listener understands the message. Listener is listening carefully.	Allows speaker to better understand the meaning of the communication. Provides for mutual understanding.
4. Responding to Feelings (Reflecting Expressed Feelings) (Responding to Subtle Feelings)	+ +	+ +	Listener is interested in the speaker's feelings. Listener is sensitive to speaker. Listener is fully understanding the message.	Personalizes the communication. Encourages speaker to express self further. Deepens trust. Deepens the relationships. Opens up communication.
5. Genuineness and Self-Disclosure	+	+	Listener wishes to share personal information. Listener is being open.	Broadens communication to two-way. Provides for understanding within the relationship.
6. Feedback	+		How the receiver is coming across to another person. Giver of feedback cares enough to take a risk.	Provides for understanding. Increases openness and honesty.
7. Confrontation	+		A high form of caring about the person and about the topic of the confrontation. Honesty and concern for the receiver.	Removes an obstacle within a relationship. Makes important issues explicit.

FIGURE 2-2. Summary of Human Relations Skills.

Egan, G. The skilled helper: A model for systematic helping and interpersonal relating. Monterey, California: Brooks/Cole Publishing, 1975.

Egan, G. You and me: The skills of communicating and relating to others. Monterey, California: Brooks/Cole, 1977.

Gazda, G. M., Asbury, F. R., Balzer, F. J., Childers, W. C., & Walters, R. P. Human relations development: A manual for educators (2nd ed.). Boston: Allyn & Bacon, 1977.

George, R. L., & Glazer-Waldman, H. Human relations skills in teaching. In N. Colangelo, C. H. Foxley, & D. Dustin (Eds.), Multicultural nonsexist education. Dubuque, Iowa: Kendall/ Hunt, 1979.

Ivey, A. E. Microcounseling, 5th printing. Springfield, Ill.: Charles C. Thomas, 1971.

SPECIAL NOTE TO INSTRUCTORS

We believe that effective communication is the foundation for discussions and exercises on racism, sexism, and other forms of prejudice and stereotyping. While we believe that the skills presented in this chapter can enhance effective communication, we are also well aware that they are culture-specific. In certain cultures these same skills would not be seen as tools for effective communication. It is important for students to recognize this, and we encourage instructors to discuss alternative means of communication that may be more effective with certain cultures. It would be against the goals of this workbook to assume that these skills are the "correct" ones or are appropriate for all cultural groups. They represent one means of communication in North American culture.

This introductory exercise enables you to discern single communication skills. It requires you to observe another teacher in action and to record your observations.

GOALS

1. To introduce the process of making specific observations
2. To enable you to discriminate among different aspects of teacher communication
3. To increase awareness of teacher communication in the classroom

DIRECTIONS

A. Select a teacher and get permission to observe him or her.
B. Explain that you are trying to familiarize yourself with certain communications skills.
C. Observe for 10 to 30 minutes and fill out the Teacher Observation Form below.
D. Repeat the assignment as desired.
E. Draw comparisons among your observations.
F. Offer to share the results with the person whom you observed.

Teacher Observation Form

Observer's name _____

Date _____

Grade/class being observed _____

Time started observation _____

Time ended observation _____

Place tally marks in the right-hand columns.

	First 10 Minutes	Next 10 Minutes	Last 10 Minutes
1. Times teacher looked at class directly			
2. Times teacher addressed individual student			
3. Times teacher addressed class in general			
4. Times teacher asked a question			
5. Times teacher answered a question			
6. Times content of a personal nature occurred			

Summary of observations

1. How representative of the individual's behavior do you believe
    your observations were? _____

    _____

    _____

    _____

    _____

    _____

2. What pattern(s) of communication emerged from your observations?

    _____

    _____

    _____

3. What recommendations do you have for the teacher based on your
    observations? _____

    _____

    _____

    _____

    _____

    _____

4. How was this classroom communication similar to your own?

    _____

    _____

    _____

    _____

5. If you observed the same teacher twice or two teachers, what
    similarities and differences did you observe? _____

    _____

    _____

    _____

    _____

18

EXERCISE 2   INCREASING SELF-AWARENESS

This exercise enables you to receive some feedback about your own communication. It requires that you have friends, coworkers, or your superiors observe and summarize your "typical" communications.

GOALS

1.   To determine your communication characteristics
2.   To learn about how your communication affects others
3.   To discover your communication tendencies that are agreed on by observers

DIRECTIONS

A.   Use the Interpersonal Communication Feedback Form to discover how an observer would characterize your communications.
B.   Select those people who know you best, who are most likely to cooperate, and who see you in different settings.
C.   Mail or give copies of the form to your observers, and ask them to complete the form and return it to you.
D.   Summarize the observations using the summary form.
E.   Consider the discussion questions at the end of this exercise.

Interpersonal Communication Feedback Form

Your name _____

Observer _____

Circle the appropriate number for all five items.

1. To what extent does _____ typically seem interested in
                          (your first name)
   your conversation?

1	2	3	4	5
Almost				
Always		Sometimes		Seldom

2. To what extent does she or he usually look at you during your
   conversations?

1	2	3	4	5
Almost				
Always		Sometimes		Seldom

3. To what extent does she or he *understand* you right away, the
   first time you say something?

1	2	3	4	5
Almost				
Always		Sometimes		Seldom

4. To what extent would you share personal feelings with her or him?

1	2	3	4	5
Almost				
Always		Sometimes		Seldom

5. To what extent does she or he communicate clearly and with
   little repetition?

1	2	3	4	5
Almost				
Always		Sometimes		Seldom

Interpersonal Communication Feedback Form

Your name _____

Observer _____

Circle the appropriate number for all five items.

1. To what extent does _____ typically seem interested in
                          (your first name)
    your conversation?

    1   2   3   4   5
    Almost
    Always   Sometimes   Seldom

2. To what extent does she or he usually look at you during your
    conversations?

    1   2   3   4   5
    Almost
    Always   Sometimes   Seldom

3. To what extent does she or he *understand* you right away, the
    first time you say something?

    1   2   3   4   5
    Almost
    Always   Sometimes   Seldom

4. To what extent would you share personal feelings with her or him?

    1   2   3   4   5
    Almost
    Always   Sometimes   Seldom

5. To what extent does she or he communicate clearly and with
    little repetition?

    1   2   3   4   5
    Almost
    Always   Sometimes   Seldom

21

Interpersonal Communication Feedback Form

Your name _____

Observer _____

Circle the appropriate number for all five items.

1. To what extent does _____ typically seem interested in
                              (your first name)
    your conversation?

    1   2   3   4   5
    Almost
    Always   Sometimes   Seldom

2. To what extent does she or he usually look at you during your
    conversations?

    1   2   3   4   5
    Almost
    Always   Sometimes   Seldom

3. To what extent does she or he *understand* you right away, the
    first time you say something?

    1   2   3   4   5
    Almost
    Always   Sometimes   Seldom

4. To what extent would you share personal feelings with her or him?

    1   2   3   4   5
    Almost
    Always   Sometimes   Seldom

5. To what extent does she or he communicate clearly and with
    little repetition?

    1   2   3   4   5
    Almost
    Always   Sometimes   Seldom

Summary Sheet for Interpersonal Communication Feedback Form

Directions: Each item on the summary sheet corresponds to an item on the feedback form. Compile the results from the forms you distributed and enter the results.

Item	Number Circled					Total	Average
	#1	#2	#3	#4	#5		
1. Interest							
2. Eye contact							
3. Understanding							
4. Trust with feelings							
5. Clarity							

Discussion

1. What is most noticeable about your results?_____
   _____
   _____

2. Are there ratings that *all* observers agreed on?_____
   _____
   _____

3. What do the observers report as your greatest strength?_____
   _____
   _____

4. Which behaviors do you wish to maintain?_____
   _____
   _____

5. Which behaviors do you wish to change?_____
   _____

6. Formulate an action plan that describes how you will change your
   behaviors or how you will try new ones._____
   _____
   _____
   _____
   _____
   _____

You could evaluate your plan by repeating this exercise in a month
or two.

EXERCISE 3   IMAGINING PERFECTION: THE IDEAL-TEACHER FANTASY

This exercise can be done in a group or alone; variations suitable for a small group are found at the end of this exercise. The purpose is to evoke specific thoughts about the "ideal" teacher.

GOALS

1. To increase familiarity with your own ideal teacher
2. To evoke visual imagery of ideal teacher/student communication
3. To stimulate group discussion about differences and similarities in ideas of the ideal teacher

DIRECTIONS   *(The following is to be read by the leader in a slow, relaxed manner.)*

A. Try to visualize as specifically and vividly as possible. Put yourself into your fantasy.
B. Relax now. Close your eyes. Get comfortable. *(Pause 15 seconds.)*
C. Picture an ideal school setting. Note the school; its location. Note the weather. See the setting vividly.
D. Notice the students. They are behaving well. They're pleasant and happy.
E. Now visualize an ideal teacher: a person who represents how you'd like to be in every respect. *(Pause one minute.)*
F. Now visualize this teacher in a classroom. Specifically watch the different things the teacher does. Notice how effectively learning takes place.
G. Now picture this ideal teacher interacting with students. The teacher is liked, trusted, respected. What is this ideal teacher doing with students? How do they interact?

Reactions to Fantasy

1. What did you learn about yourself in this exercise?

   _____

   _____

   _____

2. What did you notice about your ideals of teaching?

   _____

   _____

   _____

3. How did the ideal teacher interact with students?

   _____

   _____

   _____

4. What did the ideal teacher do that you do?

_____

_____

_____

5. What did the ideal teacher do that you seldom do?

_____

_____

_____

Discussion

A. Recall a teacher who you felt was very effective.
B. What personal and professional qualities do you remember about this teacher? _____

_____

_____

_____

C. What behaviors of this teacher do you remember as especially effective? _____

_____

_____

_____

D. Share with the group what you have been able to recall about this teacher.
E. As a group, outline a summary of the ideal teacher.
F. Discuss the implications of this composite ideal for training teachers in human relations skills.

This exercise introduces different aspects of attending and familiarizes you with examples.

GOALS

1. To stimulate your awareness of your attending behavior
2. To stimulate careful attending
3. To provide feedback about your attending behavior

DIRECTIONS

A. Recall that careful attending is indicating to the speaker that you are interested. This is done by looking at the speaker and looking interested in what the speaker is saying. Comments such as "Uh-huh" or "Really" are also an appropriate way to show attentiveness.
B. Practice before a group. Be aware of your own attending and non-attending. Use the chart below to record your behaviors.

Tally of Attending Behaviors

Setting	Attended: Yes or No	If Yes, How? What Did You Do?
1.		
2.		
3.		
4.		
5.		

C. Take turns practicing.
    1. Pick an interesting story to tell--for example, a recent trip,
        an interesting party, a funny instance in class.
    2. Watch your partner's attending behavior carefully.
    3. Stop and give your partner a description of his or her
        attending behavior.
    4. Reverse rolls.
    5. Try again.

What I learned about my own attending behavior: _____

_____

_____

_____

_____

_____

_____

D. Practice attending in a group.
    1. Take turns demonstrating careful attending while the group
        observes.
    2. Use the Observation Feedback Forms to record observations and
        give them to each participating group member.
    3. Let each member (who wishes) receive feedback.
    4. Ideas for role playing:
        a. person telling why one should or should not go into
            teaching
        b. teacher telling you that your child is a "bad" student
        c. student explaining why assignment is not in on time
        d. principal explaining why you are to take lunchroom duty
            for an entire semester
    5. Collect your observers' sheets and analyze them.

Several observers noted that I _____

_____

_____

_____

Based on observers' comments, I need to _____

_____

_____

_____

_____

Observation Feedback Form

Class observation of *(Name)*_____

Evidence of Attending

Eye contact:_____

_____

_____

_____

Looking *at* other person:_____

_____

_____

_____

Signs of interest:_____

_____

_____

_____

Different phrases used that showed interest:_____

_____

_____

_____

_____

_____

_____

_____

_____

_____

Observation Feedback Form

Class observation of *(Name)*_____

Evidence of Attending

Eye contact:_____

_____

_____

_____

Looking *at* other person:_____

_____

_____

_____

Signs of interest:_____

_____

_____

_____

Different phrases used that showed interest:_____

_____

_____

_____

_____

_____

_____

_____

_____

_____

Observation Feedback Form

Class observation of *(Name)*_____

Evidence of Attending

Eye contact:_____

_____

_____

_____

Looking *at* other person:_____

_____

_____

_____

Signs of interest:_____

_____

_____

_____

Different phrases used that showed interest:_____

_____

_____

_____

_____

_____

_____

_____

_____

_____

Special Note to Instructors

It is important to keep in mind that some communication skills reflect specific cultural values. For example, attending behavior such as eye contact may be regarded in some cultures as a sign of disrespect.

EXERCISE 5   APPLICATION OF CAREFUL ATTENDING

Careful attending is largely nonverbal. It can be communicated regardless of what a speaker says. This exercise features the application of careful attending to each participant's "typical" method of communication.

GOALS

1. To sharpen your observations of nonverbal communication
2. To stimulate your awareness of your own attending skills
3. To improve your attending skills

DIRECTIONS

A. Observe outside of class.
   1. Observe for a day or so the typical conversations of your friends, family, and other teachers.
   2. Record the careful-attending and nonattending behaviors on the Observations of Attending Form.
   3. List the various ways people show attending.
   4. Be prepared to discuss your observations with your group.
B. Practice with videotape. With a partner, televise yourself carefully attending.
   1. Describe your own attending.
      a. Reactions to self on TV:_____

      _____

      _____

      _____

      _____

      _____

      _____

      _____

      b. I need to_____

      _____

      _____

      _____

      _____

      _____

      _____

      _____

      _____

Observations of Attending Form

Careful-Attending Behaviors

	Who? Where?	Means of Expression
1.		
2.		
3.		

Nonattending Behaviors

	Who? Where?	Means of Expression
1.		
2.		
3.		

34

2. Discuss your attending with your partner.
   a. How do I express interest?_____

   _____

   _____

   b. What nonverbal signs of attending do I communicate?

   _____

   _____

   _____

3. Have a few classmates complete the Observation Feedback Form while they observe you on videotape. Discuss with the group their reactions to your attending behavior.

Observation Feedback Form

Class observation of *(Name)*_____

Attending and Nonattending Behaviors

Posture:_____

_____

_____

_____

  Barriers?_____

_____

_____

Eye contact:_____

_____

_____

_____

Movement:_____

_____

_____

_____

  Towards?_____

_____

_____

  Distractions?_____

_____

_____

Facial expression (describe):_____

_____

_____

_____

_____

_____

_____

Observation Feedback Form

Class observation of *(Name)*_____

Attending and Nonattending Behaviors

Posture:_____

_____

_____

_____

   Barriers?_____

_____

_____

Eye contact:_____

_____

_____

_____

Movement:_____

_____

_____

_____

   Towards?_____

_____

_____

   Distractions?_____

_____

_____

Facial expression (describe):_____

_____

_____

_____

_____

_____

Observation Feedback Form

Class observation of *(Name)* _____

Attending and Nonattending Behaviors

Posture: _____

_____

_____

_____

  Barriers? _____

_____

_____

Eye contact: _____

_____

_____

_____

Movement: _____

_____

_____

_____

  Towards? _____

_____

_____

  Distractions? _____

_____

_____

Facial expression (describe): _____

_____

_____

_____

_____

_____

_____

EXERCISE 6 DISCUSSION OF CAREFUL ATTENDING

Individuals, especially after completing Exercises 4 and 5, will have different opinions about the importance of a teacher's careful attending. This exercise provides an opportunity for a group discussion.

GOALS

1. To provide opportunity for you to consider the importance of attending skills for teachers
2. To consider the application of the skill of careful attending to appropriate situations
3. To allow you to compare your opinions with those of other members of the group

DIRECTIONS

A. Discuss group members' reactions to the exercises on careful attending.
B. Possible leads for consideration:
   1. In your own words, what is the purpose of careful attending?
   2. What are some possible reactions from students when a teacher carefully attends to them?
   3. As a teacher, do you want to carefully attend to *all* your students? At all times? What would be the results?
   4. As a teacher, would you be more likely to express interest in a student's recitation of the lesson or the student's personal concerns?
   5. How do you attend to others? Describe those things you do--both verbal and nonverbal--that let the other person know you are listening. Which of your attending behaviors have you found to be most effective? What attending behaviors have you found to be confusing to others? Discuss.

Personal Notes

1. During and after discussion, I learned_____

_____

_____

_____

_____

2. As a result of the discussion, I'm less certain that_____

_____

_____

_____

_____

3. As a result of the discussion, I'm curious about _____

   _____

   _____

   _____

4. I think that for me to be an effective teacher _____

   _____

   _____

   _____

   _____

The purpose of open questions is to draw out the speaker. The open question is an invitation to explore thoughts and feelings. The importance of this skill is that it encourages people to share what is on their minds rather than simply answering with a yes or no.

GOALS

1. To provide an effective means of responding to a speaker
2. To enable you to understand and practice the technique of open questions

DIRECTIONS

A. Consider the following questions.

Closed Questions	Open Questions
1. "Are things going OK?"	"How are things going?"
2. "Do you like your teacher?"	"What do you like about your teacher?"
3. "Do you understand?"	"How could I help you understand?"
4. "Does that make you feel bad?"	"How does that make you feel?"

B. Practice before the class.
   1. Try out a few questions on a friend. Ask a few closed questions. Then try a few open questions.
   2. Note the following:
      a. Which questions seemed to result in more dialogue?

      _____

      _____

      b. What similarities and differences did you notice in re-sponse to open and closed questions?_____

      _____

      _____

      _____

      _____

      _____

C. Practice in class.
   1. With a partner take turns practicing open questions.
   2. One person starts by telling a recent experience.
   3. When appropriate, try an open question--for example, "And then what happened?" or "How did that make you feel?"
   4. Stop and discuss the practice session. What was the reaction to the question?_____

      _____

      _____

How could you improve your questioning technique?_____

_____

_____

5. Reverse roles and repeat the exercise.
6. Repeat with a new story or recent experience. See if you can ask two or three open questions in one sitting.

Reaction to Practice

1. I noticed that my partner's questions_____

_____

_____

_____

_____

2. I need to_____

_____

_____

_____

_____

3. I learned_____

_____

_____

_____

_____

_____

_____

This exercise features additional practice situations in which you can receive feedback on open questions.

GOALS

1. To stimulate the use of open questions
2. To provide reactions to your open questions

DIRECTIONS

A. Practice in a group.
    1. Divide the class into two groups, one in an inner circle and the other in an outer circle. Each person in the outer group should choose one person in the inner group to observe.
    2. The inner group starts a discussion that allows open questions. Possible topics for discussion are a recent movie, a current event, or "Why I decided to be a teacher."
    3. Observers should use the Observation of Open and Closed Questions form to tally questions. When the group member you are observing asks a question, determine whether it is open or closed. Then paraphrase the question in the space labeled "Question." Below that, in the space labeled "Effect," jot down the immediate effect this question had on the group. In other words, what kind of response did this question elicit?
    4. After the discussion is completed, share your observations with the person you observed. Discuss the observations. What patterns emerged during the discussion? What insights do you have regarding using open and closed questions?
B. Practice questions while teaching.
    1. Have a friend observe you in a teaching situation for 10 to 30 minutes, using an Observation of Open and Closed Questions form.
    2. Discuss your friend's observations.

Personal Notes

How many open questions did you try?_____

_____

_____

Which reactions do you remember from the class?_____

_____

_____

_____

Which comments do you remember from your observer?_____

_____

_____

_____

What pleased you most about this practice?_____

_____

_____

_____

_____

How could you improve your use of open questions?_____

_____

_____

_____

_____

Observation of Open and Closed Questions

Observer_____

Person observed_____

Directions: Keep track of the type of question that the person you are observing asks. Place open questions in the left column and closed questions in the right column. Note the effect the question has on the group or on the discussion.

Open Question	*Closed Question*
Question	Question
Effect	Effect
Question	Question
Effect	Effect
Question	Question
Effect	Effect
Question	Question
Effect	Effect
Question	Question
Effect	Effect

Observation of Open and Closed Questions

Observer_____

Person observed_____

Directions: Keep track of the type of question that the person you
are observing asks. Place open questions in the left column and closed
questions in the right column. Note the effect the question has on
the group or on the discussion.

Open Question	*Closed Question*
Question	Question
Effect	Effect
Question	Question
Effect	Effect
Question	Question
Effect	Effect
Question	Question
Effect	Effect
Question	Question
Effect	Effect

Observation of Open and Closed Questions

Observer_____

Person observed_____

Directions: Keep track of the type of question that the person you are observing asks. Place open questions in the left column and closed questions in the right column. Note the effect the question has on the group or on the discussion.

Open Question	*Closed Question*
Question	Question
Effect	Effect
Question	Question
Effect	Effect
Question	Question
Effect	Effect
Question	Question
Effect	Effect
Question	Question
Effect	Effect

EXERCISE 9   PRACTICING RESPONDING TO CONTENT

This exercise is a series of methods of practicing the skills of restating and paraphrasing. The opportunity for feedback is progressively increased.

GOALS

1. To stimulate the practice of paraphrasing and restating
2. To suggest opportunities for practicing these skills
3. To provide feedback about your use of them

Examples of restatement.
   a. "I can't get this assignment."
       Restatement: "You can't get it, eh?"
   b. "He hit me."
       Restatement: "He hit you!"

Examples of paraphrase that are more concise and change some of the words.
   a. "Cheri hit Joel. And then all the boys started chasing me. And then Mr. Breamons called us in to the office."
       Paraphrase: "I hear you saying that because of your behavior, Mr. Breamons called you all in."
   b. "I get so tired. Sometimes all the rehearsals and challenges for my chair wear me out. I'd like to quit orchestra."
       Paraphrase: "You're questioning whether you should remain in orchestra."

DIRECTIONS

A. Practice before class.
    1. Try to restate or paraphrase the content of what a friend says.
    2. What was your friend's reaction?_____

    _____

    _____

    _____

    _____

    3. What was your reaction?_____

    _____

    _____

    _____

    _____

B. Practice in class with a partner.
    1. Have a partner tell you about a personal experience, so that you can practice the skill of paraphrasing.
    2. After two or three responses, stop and discuss them. Did your partner think your paraphrase was accurate?

3. Reactions of my partner:_____

_____

_____

_____

Ways I can improve:_____

_____

_____

_____

4. Reverse roles. You tell your partner a personal experience.
C. Continue practicing with a partner.
   1. Review point 3 above. This time as you practice, incorporate
      the feedback you received earlier.
   2. This time my partner thought_____

_____

_____

_____

_____

   3. I'd like to improve_____

_____

_____

_____

_____

   4. Reverse roles.
D. Practice with two other partners.
   1. Form groups of three. One person tells a personal experience;
      one practices paraphrasing; one observes, using the Para-
      phrase Practice Observer Form.
   2. After three or four minutes, stop and discuss the observer's
      tallies.
   3. What the observer told me:_____

_____

_____

_____

_____

I need to_____

_____

_____

_____

_____

4. Change roles. Repeat this exercise.

Paraphrase Practice Observer Form

Observer_____

Person observed_____

Directions: Write down the responses that the person gives to the person relating a personal experience. Check the paraphrases column if the response is a paraphrase. Check the other column if it is not.

Responses	Paraphrase	Other
1.		
2.		
3.		
4.		

Paraphrase Practice Observer Form

Observer_____

Person observed_____

Directions: Write down the responses that the person gives to the person relating a personal experience. Check the paraphrases column if the response is a paraphrase. Check the other column if it is not.

Responses	Paraphrase	Other
1.		
2.		
3.		
4.		

EXERCISE 10   PRACTICE OF CAREFUL ATTENDING, OPEN QUESTIONS, AND
                RESPONDING TO CONTENT

    This exercise combines the first three skills in this chapter.
Suggestions are made for practicing in three settings--in this class
or workshop, on videotape, and in another classroom.

GOALS

1. To encourage the integration of the communication skills
2. To provide feedback to you about your communication
3. To increase the transfer of learning to other settings

DIRECTIONS

A. Practice in a group.
    1. Divide the class into two groups. One group forms an inner
        circle, and the other group forms an outer circle to observe.
    2. The inner group should conduct a discussion that allows all
        group members to practice the skills of attending, asking
        questions, and responding to content.
    3. Observers should use the Integrated Observation Form to tally
        their observations.
    4. After the discussion is completed, allow time for the
        observers to get together with the students they observed to
        share information they have recorded.
    5. Reverse roles, with the outer circle of observers moving into
        the inner circle, Repeat the exercise.
    6. Record your reactions to the exercise.
        a. How many accurate paraphrases did you have?_____
        b. Overall, how do you think the practice went?_____

            _____

            _____

        c. What reaction did you get from the group?_____

            _____

            _____

B. Practice on television.
    1. Videotape yourself practicing all the skills you have covered,
        especially paraphrasing and restating.
    2. Observe yourself on replay.
    3. Have a classmate complete a tally of your skills using the
        Integrated Observation Form.
    4. From the videotape I learned_____

        _____

        _____

        _____

        _____

C. Practice while teaching.
    1. Have a classmate or a friend observe you teaching a class.
    2. Have the observer use the Integrated Observation Form.
    3. Get together after class with your observer to go over the tallies.
    4. What reactions did you get from your partner?_____

       _____

       _____

       _____

       _____

    5. How would you like to improve?_____

       _____

       _____

       _____

       _____

       _____

       _____

Integrated Observation Form

Name of person being observed_____

Observer's name_____

Directions: Check *each* time you observe your partner practicing these behavioral skills. Record your reactions in the comments column.

Careful Attending	Check	Comments
Posture		
Eye contact		
Other		
Open Questions		
Responding to Content Paraphrases		
Restatements		

General Comments:

Integrated Observation Form

Name of person being observed_____

Observer's name_____

Directions: Check *each* time you observe your partner practicing these behavioral skills. Record your reactions in the comments column.

Careful Attending	Check	Comments
Posture		
Eye contact		
Other		
Open Questions		
Responding to Content		
Paraphrases		
Restatements		

General Comments:

Integrated Observation Form

Name of person being observed_____

Observer's name_____

Directions: Check *each* time you observe your partner practicing these behavioral skills. Record your reactions in the comments column.

Careful Attending	Check	Comments
Posture		
Eye contact		
Other		
Open Questions		
Responding to Content Paraphrases		
Restatements		

General Comments:

One of the crucial skills in interpersonal relations is the ability to reflect feelings. This is the key to effective communication in the classroom.

GOALS

1. To provide a series of examples of reflecting feelings and labeling subtle feelings
2. To enable you to understand the skill of responding to feelings

DIRECTIONS

A. Review the definition of responding to feelings provided earlier in this chapter.
B. To be able to reflect a speaker's feelings, it is necessary to recognize the feelings when they are expressed. In each of the following examples note that the message contains a feeling that is explicitly expressed. Each example reflects the feeling with the same or a similar word that concretely "tags" the feeling.
   1. "Boy, things are going well. I have all my assignments in. I feel great."
       Response: "You're feeling great. You're all caught up."
   2. "I really like my teacher. She's polite, and she has a great sense of humor. I'm really glad to be in her class."
       Response: "You're pleased with your teacher."
   3. "Gee, I can't get this stuff! I work and work but I don't understand it. I feel dumb in class."
       Response: "You feel dumb when you can't get it."
   4. "I'm worried about my mom's health. She's pretty sick."
       Response: "You're concerned about your mom."
   5. "I'm really bored. There's nothing to do. All my friends are working."
       Response: "You're really bored without a job."
C. At times a speaker will indicate subtle feelings. These feelings are not expressed directly but rather seem to be right below the surface of the speaker's message. As pointed out earlier in the chapter, at times a teacher may want to label these subtle feelings. Examine the following examples of such labeling.
   1. "I don't know. I just can't remember."
       Response: "It really seems to upset you."
   2. "I have Miss Brown for my teacher. She's really polite. She treats her students with a great deal of respect. She even asks me about my other classes."
       Response: "You seem pleased to have Miss Brown as your teacher."
   3. "I'm just so busy. I have lots of homework to do. The play starts tomorrow. And of course there's my job."
       Response: "You really seem pressured by all you have to do."
   4. "I'm just so busy. I have the finals for the debate tournament coming up. Of course there's my part in the play. And then I have to preside at all the Student Council meetings."

Response: "You know, I think you're kind of proud of all
your activities."
5. "That sophomore class! They've destroyed our float and now
they won't even admit that it was them!"
Response: "You really seem angry."

This exercise contains several sections. Each provides a different means of practicing the skill of reflecting feelings.

GOALS

1. To provide opportunity for you to practice reflecting feelings
2. To stimulate the recognition of expressed feelings
3. To stimulate the reflecting of feelings
4. To provide feedback for you about your reflecting of feelings

DIRECTIONS

A. Practice before class.
   1. For the following two statements write a single "feeling word" that concretely labels the speaker's feelings. This word is the tag word. Note that there is never any *one* word that is correct. Several words will have the same effect. This exercise is intended to "sharpen your ear" for feelings. Example: "Gee, I don't know if I should. I'm worried my folks wouldn't like it. I'd hate to get caught."
      Tag word:__worried_____
      a. "I just love pets. I wish I had even more. We have a beautiful Siamese cat. She's really fun."
         Tag word:_____
      b. "I'm worried about my grades. I hope they're high enough."
         Tag word:_____
   2. For the following, write a response that accurately reflects the expressed feeling.
      a. "Gee, I feel better. I was just moping along, feeling sorry for myself. Thanks for listening."
         Response:_____

         _____

         _____

         _____

         _____

      b. "I'm so nervous about my speech. I hope I can remember it."
         Response:_____

         _____

         _____

         _____

         _____

      c. "Sometimes I hate giving grades. It's so hard to be ob-jective. I just wish teachers didn't have to give grades. It spoils the fun of teaching."
         Response:_____

         _____

B. Practice in class.
    1. Form groups of three.
        a. One of you tells a personal story that includes some feelings.
        b. One of you practices reflecting feelings.
        c. One observes and jots down the reflections that the listener tries.
        d. Share the reactions of all three of you.
        e. Shift roles and practice until everyone has had a chance at each role.
    2. Form small groups.
        a. One of you tells a story that includes some feelings.
        b. One of you practices reflecting feelings.
        c. The other members observe and give feedback to the volunteer who reflected feelings. When you give feedback, make it positive. "I like the way you . . . "
        d. Continue around the circle until everyone has reflected feelings and received feedback.
    3. Practice in two large groups.
        a. Divide the class into two groups. One group forms an inner circle, and the other group forms an outer circle to observe.
        b. The inner group should conduct a discussion that allows all members to practice reflecting feelings. Topics for discussion might be "my biggest disappointment" or "my most embarrassing moment."
        c. Observers in the outer circle should use the Reflecting Feelings Form to tally their observations.
        d. After the discussion is completed, allow time for the observers to get together with the students they observed to share the observations.
        e. Reverse roles, with the outer circle of observers moving into the inner circle. Repeat the exercise.

Reflecting Feelings Form

Name of person being observed_____

Observer_____

Directions: Jot down a very short notation or paraphrase of the
reflecting responses that the person you are observing makes. Then
note whether the reflection was accurate or inaccurate and whether it
contained a concrete feeling or tag word. Jot down the tag word.

	Reflection	Accurate/Inaccurate	Tag Word
1.			
2.			
3.			
4.			
5.			
6.			
7.			
8.			
9.			

General Comments

Reflecting Feelings Form

Name of person being observed_____

Observer_____

Directions: Jot down a very short notation or paraphrase of the reflecting responses that the person you are observing makes. Then note whether the reflection was accurate or inaccurate and whether it contained a concrete feeling or tag word. Jot down the tag word.

	Reflection	Accurate/Inaccurate	Tag Word
1.			
2.			
3.			
4.			
5.			
6.			
7.			
8.			
9.			

General Comments

EXERCISE 13   DISCUSSING THE SKILL OF REFLECTING FEELINGS

This skill is so important for effective communication that ample time is needed for you to consider reflecting feelings. Since reflecting a speaker's feelings without judging them shows the speaker that the listener cares and understands, teachers who accurately reflect feelings will find many students turning to them for assistance.

GOALS

1. To provide opportunity to hear how others feel about reflecting feelings
2. To give you a chance to express your views on the skill
3. To consider the usefulness of reflecting feelings

DIRECTIONS

A. Discuss your reactions to the exercises on reflecting feelings.
B. Consider the following questions:
   1. Is it necessary to be able to consistently reflect feelings to teach?
   2. What if sometimes I don't feel like showing someone that I understand his or her feelings?
   3. What effect on a class might it have if a teacher reflects a feeling?
   4. "I can tell how a kid feels. Why do I have to put it in words?" What is your response?
   5. How do you think a student feels when a teacher reflects a feeling accurately?
   6. When can you see yourself using this skill?

Personal Notes

1. During and after the discussion I learned_____

   _____

   _____

   _____

   _____

2. I believe my group is _____

   _____

   _____

   _____

   _____

   _____

3. I think I'm_____

_____

_____

_____

_____

4. When I practiced, I found_____

_____

_____

_____

_____

5. The feedback I got most consistently was_____

_____

_____

_____

_____

6. I think I need to _____

_____

_____

_____

_____

   A final reminder concerns those messages that contain subtle feelings. A teacher has more than one option. On the one hand, subtle
feelings can be ignored. Perhaps the time is not right for a response.
Perhaps, if the person truly wishes to be heard, the subtle feeling
will be communicated directly. On the other hand, some teachers will
wish to respond to subtle feelings. In this case teachers can ask
about the subtle feeling using an open question such as "How do you
feel about this?" Or the teacher can continue to look for further
evidence that the subtle feeling exists.

Exercises 14 through 18 cover skills that focus on teacher-initiated communication. The previous exercises were about communications made in response to others. This exercise is designed to assist participants in understanding the purposes of genuineness and self-disclosure as well as the distinctions between them.

GOALS

1. To provide examples of genuineness and self-disclosure
2. To facilitate the understanding of these two skills

DIRECTIONS

A. Recall that genuineness is defined as communicating a feeling in a concrete fashion in which the nonverbal expressions and the declared feelings of the speaker are congruent. Effective genuineness is succinct and clearly shows that the speaker is taking responsibility for the feeling ("I'm mad," as opposed to "You make me so mad"). Examine the following examples of genuineness.
    1. "I get so uptight. I'm just frustrated."
    2. "Boys, I really get nervous when you play catch with that microscope."
    3. "I'm furious."
B. Recall that the definition for self-disclosure is broader than that of genuineness. Self-disclosure is communicating any personal opinion, experience, or thought. It may or may not contain feelings. Genuineness always contains a concrete expression of feeling. Effective self-disclosures are usually short rather than rambling, and contain a purpose that is clear to the other person. Examine the following examples of self-disclosure.
    1. "It's always fun for me to start a new school year and to greet new classes."
    2. "I can't remember very many in-service meetings that were helpful to me."
C. In a human relations education, self-disclosure generally refers to statements that contain some risk for the speaker. Such statements disclose a "self" of the person, a sense of who he or she is. Such statements are usually meaningful to the speaker and are communicated in such a way that others can sense the meaningfulness of the statement. Self-disclosure can be viewed on a continuum from low-risk to high-risk statements.

```
├────────────────────────┼────────────────────────┤
Low                     Medium                   High
Risk                     Risk                    Risk
```

Place the number of each of the following personal opinions or attributes along the continuum above according to how risky you would find it to share it with a class.

1. satisfaction with the principal
2. personal religious preference
3. personal dating activities when you were 16 years old
4. preference for skirts or pants on women
5. personal health history
6. satisfaction with a class's performance on a test
7. dissatisfaction with a class's performance on an assignment
8. personal financial status

D. Discuss your placements along the continuum with others in your class.

EXERCISE 15   PRACTICING THE SKILLS OF GENUINENESS AND
               SELF-DISCLOSURE
_____

This exercise suggests several ways of practicing genuineness and self-disclosure. Opportunity for feedback is provided.

GOALS

1. To increase understanding of genuineness and self-disclosure
2. To stimulate you to practice the two skills
3. To provide opportunity for feedback about your use of genuineness and self-disclosure

DIRECTIONS

A. Practice self-disclosure in class.
   1. Select a partner. Take turns giving self-disclosures. For example, share an interest, hobby, or experience. Ask whether your self-disclosure is clear.
   2. Now form groups of three.
      a. With one of you acting as an observer, another makes a self-disclosure, and the third person paraphrases it.
      b. Check with the observer--was the self-disclosure clear? How accurate was the paraphrase?
      c. Change roles and repeat the exercise.
B. Practice genuineness in groups of three.
   1. Decide which of you will be the observer.
   2. One of you tells the third member a story that includes one or two genuine statements--for example, "I was so mad."
   3. The listener should try to reflect these feelings.
   4. Stop and discuss with the observer. Were the genuine statements concise? Were the reflections accurate?
   5. Exchange roles and continue the exercise.
C. Practice both skills in groups of four.
   1. Form two partnerships. Using the Partner Observation Form, tally all the genuine and self-disclosing statements your partner makes.
   2. One from each pair agrees to practice while the partner observes him or her. One of the actors practices self-disclosure, and the other practices paraphrasing and reflecting feelings.
   3. Stop and discuss the ratings and tallies of genuineness and self-disclosure.
   4. Exchange roles and continue to practice and observe.
D. Practice on videotape.
   1. The skills of self-disclosure and genuineness are especially good to practice on videotape, because you can observe your own nonverbal behaviors.
   2. Make a videotape of yourself teaching a short lesson that will allow you to make some self-disclosures.
   3. Use the Self-Observation Form to react to your lesson.
   4. With two other persons make arrangements to videotape the group exercises above.
   5. Use the Partner Observation Form to rate one another as you play back the videotape.

69

Partner Observation Form

Name_____

Partner's Name_____

Directions: In the top part of this form, record the genuine feelings
expressed by your partner. Also, describe the nonverbal behaviors. In
the bottom, write self-disclosure statements, write if you think the
length of the statements is about right or too long, and record your
reactions to each statement.

Genuineness	Nonverbal Behavior

Self-disclosure Statement	Length	Reaction

Partner Observation Form

Name_____

Partner's Name_____

Directions: In the top part of this form, record the genuine feelings
expressed by your partner. Also, describe the nonverbal behaviors. In
the bottom, write self-disclosure statements, write if you think the
length of the statements is about right or too long, and record your
reactions to each statement.

Genuineness	Nonverbal Behavior

Self-disclosure Statement	Length	Reaction

Partner Observation Form

Name_____

Partner's Name_____

Directions: In the top part of this form, record the genuine feelings expressed by your partner. Also, describe the nonverbal behaviors. In the bottom, write self-disclosure statements, write if you think the length of the statements is about right or too long, and record your reactions to each statement.

Genuineness	Nonverbal Behavior

Self-disclosure Statement	Length	Reaction

Self-Observation Form

Date of Videotape_____

Directions: In the top of this form, record the genuine feelings expressed by you. Also, describe your nonverbal behaviors. In the bottom part, write self-disclosure statements, write if you think the length of those statements was about right or too long, and record your reactions to each statement.

Genuineness	Nonverbal Behavior

Self-disclosure Statement	Length	Reaction

EXERCISE 16   ROLE PLAYING IN FEEDBACK SITUATIONS

Teachers are called on to give feedback every day. All too often the person giving feedback does not take into account the feelings of the person who is receiving it. This exercise provides several opportunities for practicing feedback.

GOALS

1. To stimulate your awareness of the effects of your feedback
2. To encourage effective feedback
3. To provide realistic situations in which a teacher would use feedback

DIRECTIONS

A. Form groups of three. The roles are a person practicing giving feedback, the target of feedback, and an observer. Here are some suggested situations:
   1. A principal giving feedback to a new teacher who hasn't been doing hall duty outside his or her own room.
   2. A teacher giving feedback to a girl who didn't get the lead in a play or musical.
   3. A teacher giving feedback to a parent about the misbehavior of his or her child.
   4. A teacher giving feedback to a student who keeps interrupting without raising his or her hand.
   5. Students can devise their own role-play situations.
B. Practice giving feedback while being observed, using the Feedback Observation Form.
C. Discuss the role playing.
D. Change roles and continue practicing.

Feedback Observation Form

Name of person giving feedback_____

Person observing_____

Directions: When observing feedback, write a key word or key phrase under "Feedback Example." Check whether the feedback was behavioral, such as "You looked down at the floor," and check whether the speaker included judgments such as "You were afraid of him." Note the effect of the feedback.

Feedback Example	Behavioral	Judgmental	Effects
1.			
2.			
3.			
4.			
5.			

Feedback Observation Form

Name of person giving feedback_____

Person observing_____

Directions: When observing feedback, write a key word or key phrase under "Feedback Example." Check whether the feedback was behavioral, such as "You looked down at the floor," and check whether the speaker included judgments such as "You were afraid of him." Note the effect of the feedback.

Feedback Example	Behavioral	Judgmental	Effects
1.			
2.			
3.			
4.			
5.			

Feedback Observation Form

Name of person giving feedback_____

Person observing_____

Directions: When observing feedback, write a key word or key phrase
under "Feedback Example." Check whether the feedback was behavioral,
such as "You looked down at the floor," and check whether the speaker
included judgments such as "You were afraid of him." Note the effect
of the feedback.

Feedback Example	Behavioral	Judgmental	Effects
1.			
2.			
3.			
4.			
5.			

You have been practicing several skills in small groups and with partners. This exercise requires you to recall some of those activities in order to give feedback to a partner.

GOALS

1. To provide you with behavioral feedback
2. To stimulate the practice of effective feedback

DIRECTIONS

A. Divide the class into pairs.
B. Give your partner feedback based on your observations of his or her behavior in this class.
C. Attempt to keep your feedback behavioral; avoid global judgments; try to provide specific examples.
D. Discuss your reactions to the exercise.
E. Reverse roles and repeat the exercise.
F. Discussion:
    1. Which was more difficult, giving or receiving feedback?
    2. How difficult was it to keep the feedback specific?
    3. To what extent did either of you get defensive during the exercise?
    4. How would the skill of effective feedback help a teacher?

Personal Notes

1. What I learned about myself was_____

    _____

    _____

2. My partner seemed to think I_____

    _____

    _____

    _____

3. Some of my behaviors my partner valued were_____

    _____

    _____

    _____

4. When I gave the feedback I_____

    _____

    _____

5. My feedback affected my partner by_____

    _____

    _____

The final exercise of this chapter is not a skill per se. Rather, confrontation requires that communication skills be used in a particular situation. This exercise allows participants to consider a particular teacher's use of confrontation.

GOALS

1. To stimulate consideration of appropriate use of confrontation
2. To further your understanding of confrontation

DIRECTIONS

A. Place a check by those persons you would be likely to confront.
　　　＿＿＿1. chronically tardy student
　　　＿＿＿2. meddling parent
　　　＿＿＿3. bully
　　　＿＿＿4. principal who makes sexist statements
　　　＿＿＿5. teacher who keeps putting down students
　　　＿＿＿6. student who makes racist statements
　　　＿＿＿7. teacher who frequently interrupts you
B. Discuss your responses with a partner.
C. Assess your own confrontational tendencies.
　　1. In a risk-taking situation, I usually＿＿＿＿＿＿＿＿＿＿＿＿＿＿

　　　　＿＿＿＿＿＿＿＿＿＿＿＿＿＿＿＿＿＿＿＿＿＿＿＿＿＿＿＿＿＿＿＿＿＿

　　　　＿＿＿＿＿＿＿＿＿＿＿＿＿＿＿＿＿＿＿＿＿＿＿＿＿＿＿＿＿＿＿＿＿＿

　　　　＿＿＿＿＿＿＿＿＿＿＿＿＿＿＿＿＿＿＿＿＿＿＿＿＿＿＿＿＿＿＿＿＿＿

　　2. My willingness to become involved in confrontation can best be described as＿＿＿＿＿＿＿＿＿＿＿＿＿＿＿＿＿＿＿＿＿＿＿

　　　　＿＿＿＿＿＿＿＿＿＿＿＿＿＿＿＿＿＿＿＿＿＿＿＿＿＿＿＿＿＿＿＿＿＿

　　　　＿＿＿＿＿＿＿＿＿＿＿＿＿＿＿＿＿＿＿＿＿＿＿＿＿＿＿＿＿＿＿＿＿＿

　　　　＿＿＿＿＿＿＿＿＿＿＿＿＿＿＿＿＿＿＿＿＿＿＿＿＿＿＿＿＿＿＿＿＿＿

　　3. My ability to control emotions in a confrontational situation is ＿＿＿＿＿＿＿＿＿＿＿＿＿＿＿＿＿＿＿＿＿＿＿＿＿＿＿＿＿＿

　　　　＿＿＿＿＿＿＿＿＿＿＿＿＿＿＿＿＿＿＿＿＿＿＿＿＿＿＿＿＿＿＿＿＿＿

　　　　＿＿＿＿＿＿＿＿＿＿＿＿＿＿＿＿＿＿＿＿＿＿＿＿＿＿＿＿＿＿＿＿＿＿

　　　　＿＿＿＿＿＿＿＿＿＿＿＿＿＿＿＿＿＿＿＿＿＿＿＿＿＿＿＿＿＿＿＿＿＿

　　4. My ability to use communication skills in a confrontational situation is＿＿＿＿＿＿＿＿＿＿＿＿＿＿＿＿＿＿＿＿＿＿＿＿

　　　　＿＿＿＿＿＿＿＿＿＿＿＿＿＿＿＿＿＿＿＿＿＿＿＿＿＿＿＿＿＿＿＿＿＿

　　　　＿＿＿＿＿＿＿＿＿＿＿＿＿＿＿＿＿＿＿＿＿＿＿＿＿＿＿＿＿＿＿＿＿＿

　　　　＿＿＿＿＿＿＿＿＿＿＿＿＿＿＿＿＿＿＿＿＿＿＿＿＿＿＿＿＿＿＿＿＿＿

　　5. Compare and discuss your self-assessments.

3
Recognizing and Changing Sexist Attitudes and Behaviors

INTRODUCTION

During recent years, the national news media have highlighted the women's movement's attempts to alleviate the plight of modern women. As magazines, news broadcasts, and documentaries point out, a majority of the population has frequently been treated as second class. Sexism is typically defined by stereotypic attitudes toward females. Sexism as used in this workbook, however, includes stereotypic attitudes and behaviors toward males as well.

The media exposure has resulted in some change, some resistance, and some blasé, apathetic responses, such as "Oh, no! Not this again." What is your attitude?

Each person has attitudes toward the opposite sex. People vary in the rigidity and intensity of these attitudes. They also vary in how much opportunity they have had to examine these attitudes. How long have the attitudes existed? To what extent do daily behaviors reflect these attitudes?

This chapter is designed to heighten your awareness of attitudes and behaviors. By bringing facets of the self into awareness, you can choose those that are most appropriate. Some individuals may gain insight and recall forgotten experiences that enrich their present sense of self. Some may verify a sense of satisfaction: "This is me and I am comfortable with myself. I like who I am." Some may choose to change, to alter an aspect of self. The experience of becoming more self-aware is sure to affect everyone.

The goal of this chapter is to stimulate you to explore your attitudes and behaviors regarding sex roles. Various stimuli for this personal search are suggested. Attitudes are complex, varied, and sometimes contradictory. Some private attitudes are rarely exposed to public scrutiny; others are public and, in fact, involve other people. Participating in the activities of this chapter can help you find out more about your complex response to sexism.

Educators frequently hear that sexist attitudes are prevalent in the school system. The individual men and women who educate others resemble the rest of the population in their views of sex roles. Educators with liberal attitudes coexist with conservatives. There is no doubt that some educators consciously or unconsciously perpetuate sexism. You are challenged here to search for self-knowledge about sex roles. What kind of educator are you? To what extent are you part of a problem in perpetuating sexism? To what extent are you helping to implement nonsexist solutions in education?

Behaviors may closely parallel attitudes. For example, an elementary teacher who has always thought of females as the "fairer sex" might say that "10-year-old girls are likely to spend a lot of time in front of a mirror." At other times, however, teachers' behaviors may seem totally unrelated—even contradictory—to perceived attitudes.

The exercises in this chapter offer the opportunity to examine the impact of your behavior on others. Certain activities suggest role playing and dramas that allow individuals to act in a particular situation. Sometimes just the acting allows participants to recognize their own behaviors.

In addition, group discussions let you think about the impact of certain behavior on others. You can cross-check how some acts are perceived by different participants. With encouragement and support from the group, participants can speculate on how behaviors may be affecting their professional and personal interactions. By making public a part of the self-examination process, the individual gains, and others vicariously learn about themselves.

Stereotypes occur in the area of sex-role relationships just as in all other areas of human interaction. Most individuals hold preconceived notions about certain groups of people. Therefore, most people are likely to believe in some stereotypes regarding the sexes. It is beneficial to look for personally held tendencies to stereotype as part of the self-examination process. Uncovering certain stereotypes provides opportunity to change. Choosing to discuss one's stereotypes with others allows for a richer, more varied self-study. The purpose of focusing on sex-role stereotypes is to enrich individual awareness; it is not an effort to "catch" individuals engaging in stereotyped thinking.

It is hoped that the activities of this chapter will lead to some transfer to real-life situations. Suggestions are made for classroom activities. At times participants are asked to examine classroom materials, interview a family member, or conduct other such "back home" or "back at school" activities. The effectiveness of this chapter lies in the extent to which individual educators are able to produce changes in their own work settings. Certain activities suggest a concerted, systematic effort to bring about change in the entire school or school system. Even a small nucleus of individuals can bring about widespread, lasting change.

EXERCISE 19 SELF-AWARENESS: DISCOVERING YOUR OWN IDEAS

This exercise is simply a means to record your own attitude toward sexual roles. It requires you to write down thoughts and ideas, to examine them and, perhaps, to share them with a group.

GOALS

1. To enable you to think about your attitudes
2. To increase awareness of personal values
3. To facilitate a group discussion whose participants have already thought about specific reactions and issues

DIRECTIONS

A. List several adjectives that you believe describe the typical male child._____

_____

_____

_____

_____

B. List several adjectives that you believe describe the typical female child._____

_____

_____

_____

_____

C. Consider these two lists. How different are your lists? Check the adjectives that differ the most. How similar are the lists? Circle the adjectives found on both lists.
D. List several adjectives that describe the typical male adult.

_____

_____

_____

_____

E. List several adjectives that describe the typical female adult.

_____

_____

_____

_____

_____

F. Consider your list for the typical adult of your sex. To what
    extent do you have the characteristics that you listed as typical?

    _____

    _____

    _____

    _____

    _____

G. What is your reaction to your answer to F?_____

    _____

    _____

    _____

    _____

    _____

H. What behaviors do you believe are appropriate for men but not for
    women?_____

    _____

    _____

    _____

    _____

    _____

I. What behaviors do you believe are appropriate for women but not
    for men?_____

    _____

    _____

    _____

    _____

All too often education prohibits, or attempts to prohibit, people's idle thoughts and fantasies. As a result we may "learn" to ignore some of our own experience. This exercise attempts to help you remember some of your own early experience about being a "man" or a "woman."

GOAL

To stimulate your thinking about the extent of sexism in your own upbringing

DIRECTIONS

A. Get comfortable, relax, get rid of any distractions, and think back to your own early childhood. Who told you how to behave properly? What did you learn about proper behavior for your sex? Recall for a few minutes your own early experiences about being a man or a woman.

B. Write a summary of how you were trained to be a "proper" member of your sex. _____

_____

_____

_____

_____

_____

C. What feelings has this exercise elicited in you? _____

_____

_____

_____

_____

_____

D. What would you like to do differently with your own children? ____

_____

_____

_____

_____

_____

_____

E. In rearing your own children, what would you hope to repeat from your own upbringing in instilling proper behavior for a member of your sex? _____

_____

_____

_____

_____

_____

_____

It is important for anyone who is teaching (as a profession) to think about what behaviors he or she expects from students. These expectations can give insight into one's attitudes about sex-related behaviors.

GOALS

1. To help you become aware of your expectations about student behavior based on the sex of students
2. To encourage you to share your expectations with other participants

DIRECTIONS

A. Imagine you are teaching. Think about the behavior of students in your classroom. List five behaviors you would expect from boys and five from girls.
Expected behaviors from boys:

1._____
2._____
3._____
4._____
5._____
Expected behaviors from girls:

1._____
2._____
3._____
4._____
5._____
B. How many of these behaviors are similar? Different? What insight do you have into your own attitudes based on these expected behaviors?
C. How do you think you would respond to each of these behaviors?
D. Discuss your listings with the class.

One way to understand your present attitudes about sex roles is to reflect on some of your early experiences. This reflection can clarify present attitudes and behaviors for you. Also, it can give you a rationale and direction for change.

GOALS

1. To help you clarify your attitudes about sex roles
2. To help you trace these attitudes to early family and school experiences

DIRECTIONS

A. Complete these sentences.
    1. When I was growing up, women in my family were_____

    _____

    2. When I was growing up, men in my family were_____

    _____

    3. When I was in elementary school, girls were_____

    _____

    4. When I was in elementary school, boys were_____

    _____

    5. I remember hearing that a woman should be_____

    _____

    6. I remember hearing that a man should be_____

    _____

    _____

B. After you have finished the sentence completions, form small groups and discuss them.

Discussion

1. What did you learn about your early sex-role expectations?
2. Are you surprised by any of your completions?
3. Which of these early attitudes do you still hold? Which are no longer relevant? How do you account for these changes (or lack of changes)?
4. Which of your attitudes do you think have enhanced your understanding of members of both sexes? Which of your attitudes do you think have limited your understanding of members of both sexes?
5. What people or events in your background do you think had the strongest influences on your attitudes about members of your sex? About members of the opposite sex?

Often, in our everyday living, we fail to observe the obvious. You
are asked to spend some time just observing. Try to be aware of
sexual differences and innuendos reflecting sex-role stereotypes.

GOALS

1. To become more aware of sex-role stereotypes
2. To practice the skill of observing
3. To help participants discriminate between observations and personal
    opinions and bias
4. To provide personal material for a group discussion

DIRECTIONS

A. Take a half-hour and observe children at play.
    1. List behaviors you observed.
        a. Behaviors observed in boys_____

        _____

        _____

        _____

        _____

        _____

        _____

        _____

        b. Behaviors observed in girls_____

        _____

        _____

        _____

        _____

        _____

        _____

        _____

    2. List stereotypes you observed._____

        _____

        _____

        _____

    3. What pleasant memories and thoughts did you have?_____

        _____

        _____

        _____

4. What did you observe that disturbed you?_____

_____

_____

_____

B. Take an evening and watch television.
    1. List sex-role behaviors that you observed.
        News_____

        _____

        _____

        _____

        Commercials_____

        _____

        _____

        _____

        Regular shows_____

        _____

        _____

        _____

        Movies_____

        _____

        _____

        _____

        Talk shows_____

        _____

        _____

        _____

    2. List stereotypes you observed._____

        _____

        _____

        _____

        _____

        _____

        _____

3. What did you observe that disturbed you?_____

_____

_____

_____

C. Look through some periodicals.
   1. List your observations about sex roles.
      Pictures_____

_____

_____

_____

_____

_____

      Contents_____

_____

_____

_____

_____

   2. List stereotypes that you observed._____

_____

_____

_____

_____

_____

_____

   3. What did you observe that disturbed you?_____

_____

_____

_____

D. Sample some of your textbooks.
   1. List your observations of sex roles._____

_____

_____

_____

_____

_____

2. List stereotypes you observed. _____

_____

_____

_____

_____

_____

_____

3. What did you observe that disturbed you? _____

_____

_____

_____

Personal Notes

1. Look back over the written remarks you have made. What conclusions can you draw?
2. Are there any obvious stereotypes that occur in more than one setting?
3. Do there seem to be age differences?
4. To what extent are your observations limited by you (the observer) and your biases? To what extent are your observations a product of your locality? Explain.

EXERCISE 24   INTERVIEW OF SOMEONE IN A SEX-STEREOTYPED OCCUPATION

Many people work in what is typically thought of as a stereotyped profession or occupation without considering the stereotyped nature of the work. Others are forced to accept employment in a position not of their choice. This exercise is designed to force you to broaden your experience and to test your own preconceived notions of men and women at work.

GOALS

1. To provide the opportunity to meet someone new
2. To test certain preconceived ideas about "appropriate" employment
3. To provide material for a class discussion or paper

DIRECTIONS

A. Select an occupation that you see as sexually stereotyped, such as bellhop, waitress, bus driver, construction worker, or secretary.
B. Conduct an interview with a person in this occupation. Sample interview questions:
1. To what extent do your customers/clients see you as a person? To what extent in a role (that is, secretary, teacher, and the like)?
2. How does this affect your attitude?
3. To what extent do you see those with whom you deal as people? To what extent do you see them as a series of demands or as deadlines for you to meet?
4. What led you to this occupation?
5. What do you enjoy about it?
6. Would you recommend this job for your daughter? Son?
C. Write a summary of what you learned. Include your personal reactions.

EXERCISE 25   SEX-ROLE ATTITUDES

   Many of us are frequently "dictated" to by our own ideas of right
and wrong. Individuals vary in the intensity of their personal feelings of right and wrong. Rarely are individuals allowed a chance to
carefully examine their own list of "shoulds" and "should nots."

GOALS

1. To stimulate personal examination
2. To provide opportunity to compare right and wrong in personal and
   professional roles

DIRECTIONS

A. Complete the following statements.

   1. Little girls must always_____

   _____

   _____

   2. Little boys must always_____

   _____

   _____

   3. Good little girls should be careful to_____

   _____

   _____

   4. Good little boys should always_____

   _____

   _____

   5. As an effective (man/woman) I must _____

   _____

   _____

   6. To be my best as a (man/woman) I have to_____

   _____

   _____

   7. Ideally, a (man/woman) should_____

   _____

   _____

   8. In my job:
       a feminine woman should_____

   _____

   _____

99

a masculine man should_____

_____

_____

my own masculinity should be_____

_____

_____

my own femininity should be_____

_____

_____

9. As a total person:
    my own masculinity helps me_____

_____

_____

    my own femininity helps me_____

_____

_____

B. Discuss your responses.

Many times males and females are not aware of their differences and similarities. Often these factors are "assumed." People can improve their communication by better understanding some of these similarities and differences.

GOALS

1. To help you become more aware of similarities to and differences from the opposite sex
2. To discuss these similarities and differences with a person of the opposite sex

DIRECTIONS

A. Form a partnership with a person of the opposite sex. Discuss with your partner differences between you because of gender. List the differences in Figure 3-1. Then discuss similarities with your partner. Jointly list these in Figure 3-2.

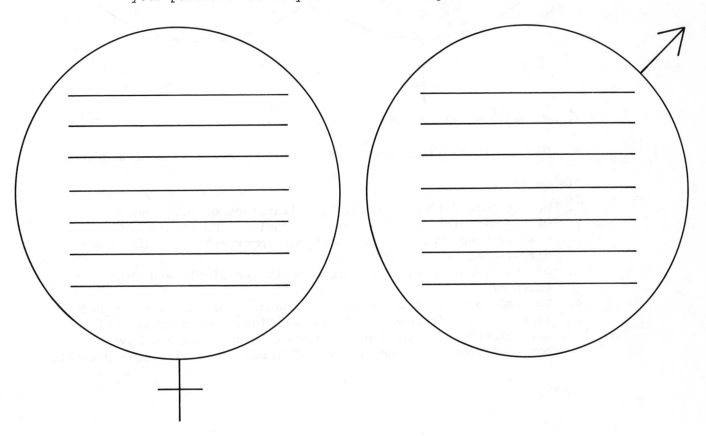

FIGURE 3-1. Differences between Partners.

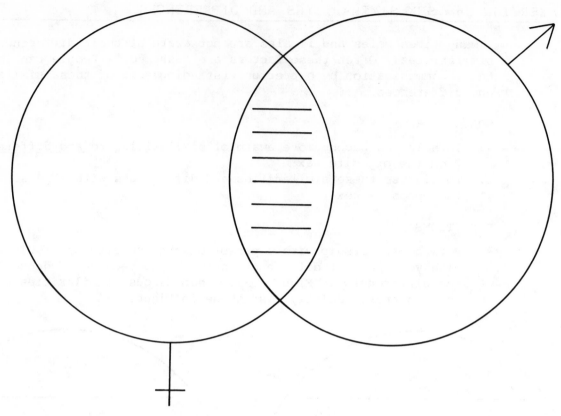

FIGURE 3-2. Similarities between Partners.

B. Discuss these lists using the questions that follow as a guide.

Discussion

1. Was it more difficult to list similarities or differences? Why?
2. Of the differences, which do you consider important? Of the similarities, which do you consider important? Are there more differences or similarities?
3. Of the differences, which are genetic (physical) and which are learned?
4. You and your partner may want to change some of your original listings of differences and similarities. How does it feel to more clearly realize that you are different from yet have commonalities with your partner? Discuss this with your partner.

One way to get acquainted with a small group is to share some ideas about yourself, including some of your attitudes.

GOALS

1. To stimulate discussion about the opposite sex
2. To provide opportunity for you to disclose some of your own attitudes about sex roles

DIRECTIONS

A. Complete the following statements.

1. Women are lucky, because they_____

    _____

    _____

2. Women have it easy, because men_____

    _____

    _____

3. Men are lucky, because they_____

    _____

    _____

4. Men have it easy, because women_____

    _____

    _____

5. Sometimes I wish I were a (man/woman), because then I_____

    _____

    _____

    _____

6. I'm glad I'm a (man/woman), because I_____

    _____

    _____

7. Too often men_____

    _____

    _____

8. Too often women_____

    _____

    _____

B. Share your answers in the group. You may want to write on a board the similarities that emerge.

Personal Notes

1. What did you notice about your own answers? _____

    _____

    _____

    _____

2. Which answers of yours most resembled those of the rest of the group? _____

    _____

    _____

    _____

3. How did you feel during the group discussion? _____

    _____

    _____

    _____

4. Did you express these feelings? Why or why not? _____

    _____

    _____

    _____

5. What did you learn from this exercise? _____

    _____

    _____

    _____

    _____

All too often our knowledge about the other sex is limited by a lack of communication. What if members of one sex felt comfortable in asking questions of the other sex?

GOALS

1. To open up communication within the class or training group
2. To increase knowledge about the opposite sex
3. To stimulate discussion within the group

DIRECTIONS

A. Write on separate slips of paper as many questions for the opposite sex as you wish. Have the women deposit their questions into one container and the men put theirs into another one.
B. Draw out questions one at a time, alternating between the two containers, and read them aloud.
C. Any member of the sex that is being questioned may answer. Allow as many different members of the sex to give an answer as wish to.

EXERCISE 29   SEX-STEREOTYPE FANTASY

This exercise allows you to experience yourself as a member of the other sex. You will be given time to imagine yourself going through a typical day in this new role.

GOALS

1. To gain an increased awareness of attitudes toward the opposite sex
2. To explore attitudes towards the opposite sex

DIRECTIONS

A. The instructor will assign to women a sex-stereotyped role such as "macho male," who is aggressive and in control, and to men a role such as a coquettish female, charming and manipulative.
B. Fantasize yourself as the person you are assigned.
C. Allow 15 minutes to "go through" the fantasy.
D. Sample leads that the instructor could give:
    1. Imagine yourself as the assigned stereotype.
    2. How do you look?
    3. What is your attitude toward your body?
    4. What were some of your typical experiences while you were in school?
    5. What are some of your typical daily activities?
    6. What problems do you face in this stereotyped role?
    7. In your stereotyped role, what would be your typical attitudes toward marriage? children? the opposite sex? domestic tasks? occupational roles?
    8. How could this stereotyped person be different five years from now?

Personal Notes

1. What reactions did you have to the fantasy?_____

    _____

    _____

    _____

    _____

2. What did you enjoy about this person and his or her life?_____

    _____

    _____

    _____

    _____

3. What made it difficult for you to "be" this person?_____

_____

_____

_____

_____

One way to get to know more about other members in your group is to share ideas about the future. As you fill in the following, try to force yourself to specify the future. As you share individual guesses about the future with other group members, you should find out more about your own attitudes and about the group.

GOALS

1. To become more aware of individual views of the future
2. To increase personal awareness about sexism
3. To stimulate discussion among group members
4. To learn about other group members

DIRECTIONS

A. Fill out the following as specifically as you can. Imagine the future 50 or 100 years from now.

   1. What will life be like in 100 years?_____

       _____

       _____

       _____

       _____

       _____

   2. If you have children, how old will they be in 50 years?_____
       What will their lives be like?_____

       _____

       _____

       _____

       _____

   3. In what ways will child care be different?_____

       _____

       _____

       _____

       _____

       _____

4. In what ways will parenthood be different?_____

_____

_____

_____

_____

5. What roles in society do you think will be differentiated by sex?_____

_____

_____

_____

_____

6. What roles in society do you think will not be differentiated by sex?_____

_____

_____

_____

_____

7. What do you predict for the institution of marriage?_____

_____

_____

_____

_____

8. What will dating and courtship be like?_____

_____

_____

_____

_____

9. What types of work will men and women be doing?_____

    _____

    _____

    _____

    _____

    _____

B. Share your answers with the group.

Role playing is different from a discussion in that participants agree to act out a certain role. Individuals attempt to react to each other as if they were the designated person in the role. In the following examples, allow plenty of time for discussion and reaction by the entire group, participants, and observers. The point is not to finish a skit but to allow members to explore their reactions.

GOALS

1. To provide opportunity for you to become involved in a selected situation
2. To stimulate group discussion and group exploration of sex-role stereotypes toward a commonly observed situation
3. To elicit sharing of personal attitudes

DIRECTIONS

Situation A: A Flat Tire. Each of us is familiar with the stereo-type of the mechanically helpless female. In the following two skits you will be given an opportunity to experience this common stereotype. Through an analysis of the role players and a discussion with the group, you will become better able to recognize your own attitudes.

Version 1. A female should move her chair to the front of the room so that it becomes her "car." She has a flat tire along a highway. Have a male play a truck driver who stops.

Version 2. In this skit have a female play the male truck driver who stops, and have a male member of the group play the helpless woman with a flat tire.

Discussion

1. After each version, discuss:
    a. What stereotypes were observed?
    b. What form did the stereotypes take?
    c. Was one of the role players more "stereotypical" than the other?
    d. What reactions to the skit and observations could be agreed on by all the observers?
    e. Which reactions or observations elicited disagreement among the observers?
    f. What general learning seems to have occurred?
    g. What did each individual learn from this exercise?
    h. What were the feelings of those playing the roles?
2. After both versions have been performed, consider:
    a. What differences were observed between the two skits?
    b. What similarities occurred in both versions?
    c. Discuss the behaviors of a truck driver and a helpless woman within the framework of your particular group. Is your group similar to other groups? Were there nonprofessionals in your group?

Situation B: Asking for a Date. Many of us accept certain tradi-tional behaviors in the areas of courtship and dating without question. Some of these "traditions" have become stereotyped. In the following skits you will be given the opportunity to compare the similarities and some differences between the sexes in the traditional area of asking for a date.

Version 1. Set the stage for this skit by determining the age of the daters and where the invitation takes place. Have the male ask the female for the first date.

Version 2. Allow the role players to determine their age and where the invitation takes place. Have the female ask the male for a first date.

Discussion

After each skit discuss:
1. What stereotypes were observed?
2. What form did the stereotypes take in the skit?
3. Was one role player more "stereotypical" than the other?
4. What reactions or observations could be agreed on by all the observers?
5. Which reactions or observations elicited disagreement among the observers?
6. What general learning seems to have occurred?

Situation C: The Job Interview. In this skit the group gets to consider the very stereotyped situation of a busy, powerful "boss" who interviews an applicant for a job. However, in this case the boss is female and the applicant is male. Decide within the group whether this is a school with a principal or a large company with an executive.

Discussion

1. What stereotypes were observed?
2. What form did they take in the skit?
3. Was one role player more "stereotypical" than the other?
4. What reactions or observations are agreed on by all the observers?
5. Which reactions or observations elicited disagreement among the observers?
6. What general learning seems to have occurred?
7. What did each individual learn from this exercise?

Sociodrama differs from a discussion in that you get up and use your whole body and sometimes props. You put yourselves into a certain situation and then play out the skit as if you were engaged in a real situation. Frequently, the same situation is repeated with different participants playing key roles. After some discussion by the entire group, it may be desirable to replay the scene without certain stereotypes. These exercises allow the exploration of attitudes and feeling with more personal participation and with more depth than earlier exercises.

Note to Instructor: It is important in this exercise that participants be given the choice of whether to participate.

GOALS

1. To allow you to experience the attitudes of characters in a specific situation
2. To provide observers with vicarious involvement in a specific situation
3. To stimulate group discussion about specific behaviors and reactions to these behaviors in a commonly observed specific instance
4. To enable you to take turns as characters in the situations and learn the effects of different behaviors in the same situation

DIRECTIONS

Scene A: A Bar. Two or three males are at a table. A female cocktail waitress is waiting on them. Allow the scene to unfold with one of the males encouraging the others to make a pass at the waitress. This scene can be reversed, with three females at a table making passes at a male waiter.

Scene B: A Laundromat. A man in a laundromat doesn't know how to sort clothes or how to work the machine. A woman responds by helping him. This scene can also be played with a woman as the helpless male and a male as the helpful woman.

Scene C: A Courtroom. This is a rape trial. Characters should include the defendant, his lawyer, the judge, and the victim. The defendant's lawyer should act out the typical strategies to cast doubt on the claim of the rape victim.

Scene D: A Judge's Chambers. This is a hearing in a divorce proceeding. Characters include the wife, her lawyer, the husband, his lawyer, and the judge. The judge should ask about such matters as custody of the children, alimony, handling of property, and the holdings left to the couple by the wife's father.

Discussion

1. What stereotypes of sex roles were obvious in the scene as enacted?
2. To what extent have the observers witnessed a similar scene in real life?
3. If more than one scene was used, were there common female

characteristics that appeared in more than one scene? Were
certain male characteristics observed in more than one scene?

4. What would have happened if you had acted out a scene of your own
group participating in a discussion? Are certain stereotyped
behaviors obvious in your own group?

5. Record your own reactions to the sociodrama exercise when you
have a chance to think about what happened.

Sometimes it's easier to talk about bias and non-bias than to actually experience a real situation. In this exercise half the time is spent simulating a situation with a dictatorial female executive; the second half of the time is spent discussing what happened.

GOALS

1. To expose you to the concept of power in a small group
2. To stimulate individual awareness
3. To provide a common stimulus for discussion
4. To distinguish between sex-related factors (female executive) and behavior-related factors (arbitrary decisions)

DIRECTIONS

A. Select the youngest female as the executive.
B. She is now to conduct a group meeting for half the time allotted for this activity.
C. The executive should conduct a discussion on a topic such as "nonproductive attitudes of certain members of this group" or "ways our group could be more effective."
D. Early in the discussion she should tell the oldest-appearing male to take notes.
E. The executive sends the heaviest person to a car to get something (a map, for example).
F. She arbitrarily ends the meeting.
G. Spend half the allotted time discussing what happened.

Discussion

1. How did individuals feel during the activity?
2. What feedback does the group have for individual members?
3. How arbitrary was the executive?
4. What was the group members' reaction to her?
5. How similar or dissimilar was the group's behavior during this activity to its behavior in earlier exercises?

Publishers have recently sought to remove the most flagrant examples of sex bias from texts. How successful have they been? What about teacher-made handouts for classroom use?

GOALS

1. To provide opportunity for you to examine your own materials and texts
2. To stimulate increased awareness about sexist language in class-room materials
3. To provide opportunity for discussion about how to overcome and change sexist materials

DIRECTIONS

A. Bring at least two texts plus samples of handouts from your own areas.
B. Start by examining sexism in language, such as "mankind"; "The senator, he . . ."; "The teacher, she . . ." Some sample counts of sexist language could be taken.
C. Look at any drawings and pictures. How many are of males? Females? Both? What are the activities in each?
D. In mathematics word problems, how many boys and how many girls are there? What are the activities of each?
E. In literature, what proportion of stories is about males? About females? What are the activities of each?
F. Allow time for members to mingle during the material examination.
G. Share the findings as a group.
H. Discuss how you can change or work around sexist materials.

Each of us has read about sexism in language and media, but how much actual observation has been done?

GOALS

1. To gather specific information about sex-role stereotyping in the media
2. To stimulate your awareness of media influence on sex-role stereotyping
3. To stimulate group discussion

DIRECTIONS

A. Decide among yourselves who is to bring toy catalogues, newspapers, magazines, and so on.
B. Before your group meeting, examine these for sex-role stereotypes.
C. Summarize your examples and at the group meeting share what you found.
D. Discuss the implications of the shared information.
E. Collect summary statements of the information gathered.
F. Finally, tell the group: "Today, I learned . . ."

EXERCISE 36   MADISON AVENUE AND SEXISM

Some commercials and advertisements feature blatant appeals to buy certain products, while others use subtle means of persuasion.

GOALS

1. To stimulate awareness of sexism in advertisements
2. To help you consider criteria for nonsexist advertisements

DIRECTIONS

A. In 10 to 20 minutes, brainstorm and summarize what criteria make up a nonsexist advertisement.
B. In a short time, collect criteria for what makes an advertisement sexist.
C. Each of you brings an example of a sexist and a nonsexist advertisement to the next meeting.
D. Discuss the examples.
E. Look again at the group criteria. What changes would you make in the criteria for sexist and nonsexist advertisements?

EXERCISE 37   WHAT IF SEX STEREOTYPES WERE ELIMINATED IN MY SCHOOL?

No doubt a sudden elimination of all traces of sexism would have many effects on a school. This exercise encourages participants to think about the changes that would result.

GOALS

1. To specify all possible effects of the sudden abolishing of sexism
2. To discuss negative and positive results of such a change

DIRECTIONS

A. In groups of four or five, list all the results that would occur if sexism in all forms were suddenly eliminated in your school.
B. Have a person record all the changes.
C. When finished, decide which changes would be positive and which negative.
D. Share your lists with other groups.

As indicated in the introduction to this chapter, one measure of the effectiveness of increased awareness of sexist attitudes and behaviors is the extent to which educators apply what they have learned to their own classrooms and school systems.

GOALS

1. To identify a sexist policy or practice in your own school
2. To identify the forces for and against changing the sexist policy or practice
3. To identify actual steps for planned change

DIRECTIONS

A. Describe a sexist policy or practice that now exists in your school. Some possibilities might be classroom behavior of you or your students, the use of sexist textbooks, sexist curricular requirements, extracurricular activities and programs that follow traditional sex-roles (for example, all-female pep club or all-male band), or staffing patterns of school personnel._____

_____

_____

_____

_____

_____

_____

B. What are the forces for and against changing this policy or practice? Such forces may be individuals, traditions, budgetary constraints, federal or state laws and regulations, and so forth. Be as specific as you can in identifying these forces.

Forces for Change	Forces Against Change
_____	_____
_____	_____
_____	_____
_____	_____
_____	_____

C. List the steps you plan to take to change this sexist policy or practice. Keep in mind the forces for and against change that you listed above. Utilize the forces for change in combatting the forces against change.

Step 1:_____

_____

Step 2:_____

_____

Step 3:_____

_____

Step 4:_____

_____

Step 5:_____

_____

Step 6:_____

_____

Step 7:_____

_____

Step 8:_____

_____

Additional steps may be listed on a separate sheet of paper if necessary.

D. Establish a timetable for the completion of each step. Be as realistic as possible. Remember that effective change usually occurs slowly.

Step 1 date of completion:_____

Step 2 date of completion:_____

Step 3 date of completion:_____

Step 4 date of completion:_____

Step 5 date of completion:_____

Step 6 date of completion:_____

Step 7 date of completion:_____

Step 8 date of completion:_____

E. Share your action plan with others to get their reactions and suggestions.

4
Recognizing and Diminishing Cultural and Racial Biases

INTRODUCTION

One of the significant characteristics of education in the 1980s will be an increased awareness of the cultural and racial diversity of students. While cultural heterogeneity has long been an element in North American schools, the traditional approach to dealing with this issue was the "melting pot." The school was expected to assimilate students of diverse backgrounds into an "anglicized" homogeneity. The concept of the melting pot has not been expounded since the late 1960s. Schools in the last decade or so have been letting go of that assimilation myth. What schools are faced with today and certainly in the immediate future, moreover, is a firm and aggressive affirmation of cultural and racial differences. Evidence of this affirmation can be found in the increased attention given to human relations training for teachers. Some states (for example, Iowa, Minnesota, Wisconsin) have mandated a human relations component as part of teacher certification.

Cultural diversity will be a key issue in the future of North American education. For teachers to be successful in their profession, it will no longer be sufficient for them to have knowledge of their subject area and basic communication skills. It will also be necessary for them to have knowledge about different cultures as well as experience and skill in communicating with culturally diverse students.

It is not enough simply to say "I accept people of all cultures." This blanket and often superficial acceptance will not meet the demands of multicultural education. What is needed is an active examination of one's attitudes and beliefs about different cultures. In addition, teachers need to engage actively in learning about the history and values of different cultures. It is this *knowledge* and *active* involvement that must differentiate the promise of multicultural education from mere cultural acceptance.

The exercises and activities in this chapter are designed to help you explore your attitudes about culture and race. They provide the opportunity for class interaction, so that participants not only receive feedback about their attitudes and behaviors but also can listen to and consider the attitudes of others.

Stereotypes about culture and race are based on limited and biased information. This information is typically not first-hand knowledge

and experience. Also, stereotypes are based on unexamined attitudes.
If change is to occur, it is imperative that people actively examine
their attitudes.

It is hoped that the exercises and activities in this chapter will
stimulate you to examine and reconsider the merits of your attitudes
about culture and ethnicity. It is assumed that all of us have
adopted some attitudes that we might wish to change. This is natural,
since as youngsters we formed some attitudes that we continue to
harbor. Our own limited interactions with our world can bias our
perceptions. Society has undergone extensive changes recently, and
we need to examine the effect of these changes on ourselves.

We believe that you can most fruitfully use this chapter by interacting honestly and openly with others in group activities. To
profess beliefs you feel are "appropriate" rather than honest will
only interfere with the process of change. It is extremely important
for the instructor to establish an atmosphere of trust, so that
students can make full use of these exercises and activities. Such
an atmosphere will enhance growth opportunities for students. Also,
it is anticipated that what people learn and practice in the classroom
will generalize to situations outside the classroom.

People often associate certain emotions, morals, values, or attitudes with colors. For example, red is associated with anger or embarrassment, blue with sadness or depression, and white with purity or goodness. This exercise stimulates discussion on color associations.

GOALS

1. To provide an opportunity for you to explore associations you have with color
2. To stimulate discussion of attitudes based on color
3. To stimulate discussion of attitudes toward people with different skin color

DIRECTIONS

A. List under White, Brown, and Black the associations that come to mind using one-word descriptors.

White	Brown	Black

B. Once you have completed your lists, put a plus (+) next to those you view as positive descriptors, a minus (-) next to those that are negative, and a zero (0) next to those that are neutral.
C. Count your (+)s, (-)s, and (0)s. What pattern has emerged?
D. Get together in small groups and discuss your patterns. What do they indicate about the potential attitudes toward people of White, Brown, or Black skin color?
E. This exercise can be expanded to include other colors (for example, red, yellow).

It is very simple to categorize people by groups. This exercise is designed to help you explore how assumptions about people in groups can be formed.

GOALS

1. To give you an opportunity to experience being labeled within a group
2. To help you examine how opinions about groups can be formed on limited or irrelevant information
3. To stimulate you to think more clearly about any individual within a group

DIRECTIONS *The instructor should pass out an envelope filled with balloons. The balloons should be of different shape or color, so that several groups can be formed.*

A. Each of you picks a balloon from the envelope.
B. Blow up the balloons and then group yourselves with others who have the same shape or color balloon.
C. In the groups make a list of assumptions about your own group and the other groups, based on the color of the balloons.
D. After these assumptions are written, all the groups come together and discuss their assumptions.

Discussion

1. What implications do these assumptions about your own group and stereotypes about people in other groups have for you?
2. How did it feel being labeled?
3. What did you learn regarding how people make assumptions about other people?

Most of us can remember how we viewed race and culture as young-sters. In this exercise you are encouraged to look at how your attitudes have changed.

GOALS

1. To help you explore changes in attitudes about race and culture
2. To help you understand what evidence you have for your attitudes as well as how this evidence has changed

DIRECTIONS

A. Complete the Attitudes about Race and Culture form.
B. Discuss your answers in small groups using the questions below as a guide.

Discussion

1. Which attitudes have changed? Which have endured? What patterns emerge in the group?
2. What evidence has been used to support attitudes? How has this changed or endured?
3. How can you account for changes in attitudes?
4. Looking at your current attitudes, if there are any that you wish to change, what is needed for change to occur?

Attitudes about Race and Culture

Age	Attitudes	Evidence (parent told me, I read it, it is rational, other)
Early childhood (through sixth grade)		
Adolescence (through high school)		
Young adult (college to age 30)		
Mid-life (30 to 50 years)		
Older age (50 years and older)		

This exercise helps you explore attitudes about race and how they may have originated in your family.

GOAL

1. To help you explore early family influence on your attitudes about race
2. To help examine the relevance of these attitudes to your current life

DIRECTIONS

A. Complete the sentences. Use a specific racial or cultural group (for example, Blacks, Chicanos, Italians, Jews).

1. When I was growing up, _____ were seen as _____

_____

_____

2. I recall that in my family _____ were talked about as

_____

_____

3. The amount of actual contact my family had with _____ was _____

_____

_____

4. As an adult my views about _____ are (similar) (different) from those of my family in the following ways:____

_____

_____

5. My children will learn that _____ are _____

_____

_____

B. Discuss your answers in small groups. What conclusions can you reach?

EXERCISE 43   PREJUDICE AND STEREOTYPES

An important first step in changing prejudices and stereotypes is to recognize these beliefs within yourself. This exercise is designed to help you identify them. *Allow time to think about this exercise before participating.*

GOALS

1. To help you identify prejudices and stereotypes
2. To help you understand the sources of your beliefs

DIRECTIONS

A. List some prejudices or stereotypes about a particular racial or cultural group that you have.

_____

_____

_____

_____

_____

B. Recall when you first held these beliefs.

_____

_____

_____

_____

_____

C. What evidence do you have to support your beliefs?

_____

_____

_____

_____

_____

D. Have you had any recent experiences that affirm or contradict your beliefs?

_____

_____

_____

_____

_____

E. Discuss your answers in small groups.

Discussion

1. What patterns of prejudice and stereotypes and their sources emerge from the group discussions?
2. What kinds of experience affirm or contradict people's beliefs?

Every month events occur that are important to various cultures. This activity is designed to highlight these events and help students better understand the contributions of different cultures.

GOALS

1. To provide you an opportunity to gain knowledge about different cultures
2. To help you understand the numerous events important to cultures

DIRECTIONS

A. This activity can be done individually or in groups. Individuals or groups can choose a month and develop a calendar that focuses on people and events of a particular ethnic group. For instance, January could be used for significant people and events of Afro-American culture, February for Puerto Ricans, March for Native Americans, and so on.
B. At the end of each month or semester the class can discuss the contributions of people of all ethnic backgrounds. It is usually helpful to realize the number of events that are important to a culture in any given month. Many students are not aware of important events for cultures other than their own.

Understanding of various cultures can be improved by stressing similarities and differences.

GOALS

1. To help you better define what similarities and differences you have with others
2. To help you realize that people, no matter how different they seem, have some similarities to others
3. To help you recognize that differences do not necessarily hamper communication or understanding

DIRECTIONS

A. Work in pairs (one person is A, the other B).
B. Share some information about yourself.
C. List those things you two see as differences in the appropriate area on the diagram below.
D. In Area C list things that are similar.

Discussion

1. From what has been listed you should choose differences and similarities that you consider most important. What conclusions can be drawn from these?
2. You should discuss what attributes could foster communication and which could hamper it. What could be done to overcome the attributes that hamper communication?

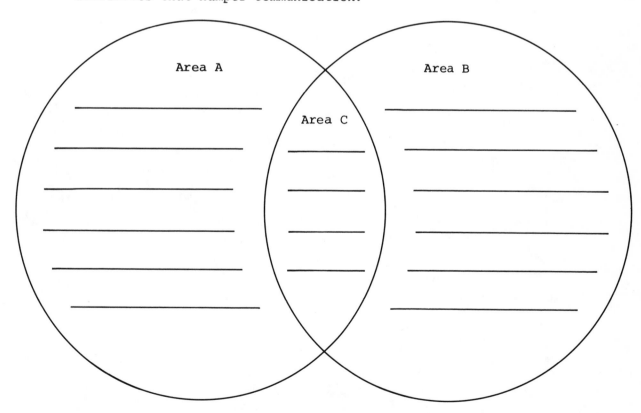

People are not always aware of their attitudes about racism. This exercise provides an opportunity to correct this situation.

GOALS

1. To explore your attitudes about racism
2. To give you a chance to evaluate your attitudes

DIRECTIONS

A. In the Racial Attitudes Form list the words or phrases that come to mind when you think about racism. List them from most important to least important.
B. Next to each one, list the evidence you have for holding this attitude or belief (for example, actual experience, reading, a movie, friends' beliefs).

Discussion

1. What patterns do you see in your attitudes about racism?
2. What kinds of evidence do you have for your beliefs?
3. How can you gather new evidence to validate or change beliefs?
4. Discuss findings as a class.

Racial Attitudes Form

	Racism		Evidence
Most Important			
Least Important			

This exercise will help you examine possible racism in local newspapers.

GOALS

1. To have you look closely at how newspapers deal with race
2. To help you better understand how covert forms of racism can pervade newspapers

DIRECTIONS

A. Use one copy of the local newspaper to answer the following:
   1. News. In many newspapers, the first three pages contain what are generally considered the most important news stories of the day.
      a. How many stories on the first three pages are mainly about Whites? _____
      b. How many stories on the first three pages are mainly about non-Whites? _____
      c. What did the non-Whites who appear on the first three pages do to cause the newspaper to write about them?

      _____

      _____

      _____

      d. What did the Whites who appear on the first three pages do that resulted in an article?_____

      _____

      _____

      _____

   2. Newsphotos. Look through the entire paper for news photographs (do not count advertisements), and answer the following:
      a. How many feature Whites as the main subject? _____
      b. How many feature non-Whites as the main subject? _____
      c. What roles (for example, politician, ballplayer, witness) do the pictures show for the non-Whites?_____

      _____

      _____

      What roles do the pictures show for the Whites?_____

      _____

      _____

   3. Movies. Use the movie listings to determine the following:
      a. How many movies star Whites only? _____
      b. How many movies star non-Whites only? _____
      c. How many movies star both Whites and non-Whites? _____

Discussion

1. As a class, discuss your findings.
2. What statements and implications can be made from the findings?
3. How accurately do the newspapers reflect the racial makeup of the community?

What messages about race can be inferred from the racial makeup of those who present the news on television?

Special note to instructors: Exercises 48, 49, and 50 all provide an opportunity to examine attitudes about race as presented on television. If a class is relatively large, we suggest that the instructor divide it into three groups and assign one exercise per group. Then the entire class can discuss and compare findings based on the three exercises.

GOALS

1. To have you closely examine the racial mix of those who present television news
2. To help you draw implications based on that racial mix

DIRECTIONS

A. Watch parts of local and national news programs during a week and fill in the Television News Form below.
B. Discuss your findings.

Discussion

1. How many of the newspeople observed were White? Non-White?
2. What roles did the non-Whites perform on the news broadcasts?
3. Were there differences between the local and national news?
4. As a class, discuss the findings. Is the racial or cultural proportion of newscasters found in the local news consistent with the racial or cultural makeup of the community?

Television News Form

Number of Newscasters Observed	Newscasters Who Were White	Newscasters Who Were Non-White (record actual race or culture)
Anchor_____	_____	_____
Weather _____	_____	_____
Sports _____	_____	_____
Editorials _____	_____	_____
Others _____	_____	_____
_____	_____	_____
_____	_____	_____
Total _____	Total _____	Total _____

This exercise is designed to examine the kinds of messages television gives regarding various cultures.

GOALS

1. To examine typical television shows in terms of ethnic and cultural portrayals
2. To examine patterns in television entertainment regarding ethnic groups and cultures

DIRECTIONS

A. Each of you is to watch a night of television broadcasts. It would be most beneficial if the class can decide who will watch which stations and which nights, so that over a week's time all nights and stations are covered.
B. After your observations answer the following:
   1. In the shows you watched, what ethnic groups were featured?

   _____

   _____

   _____

   2. What kinds of shows featured particular ethnic groups (for example, comedy, variety, talk shows, police, dramas, specials)?

   _____

   _____

   _____

   3. Based on your observations of television shows, what statements can you make concerning various racial and cultural groups you observed?

   _____

   _____

   _____

   _____

Discussion

1. To what extent is television accurate in portraying the truth about various ethnic groups?
2. What evidence could be cited to verify the accuracy or inaccuracy?

This exercise will help you examine commercials and their intended audience.

GOALS

1. To have you identify the racial or cultural makeup of characters in commercials
2. To help you think about the intended buyers at whom commercials are aimed

DIRECTIONS

A. Observe television commercials for an evening and then discuss the following:
   1. How many commercials did you observe? _____
   2. How many commercials had only White characters? _____
   3. How many commercials had non-White characters *only*? Also, what racial or cultural groups were represented? _____
      _____
      _____
   4. How many commercials included both White and non-White characters? _____
   5. Going back over questions 2, 3, and 4, what kind of product was advertised? What assumptions about income level can be inferred from the product? _____
      _____
      _____
   6. Was there any relation between the kind of product (cars, dishwashers, hamburgers, cologne) and the racial makeup of the characters in the commercial? _____
      _____
      _____

B. Discuss in groups or as a class the overall findings from this survey.

It is important for you to examine textbooks and other instructional materials that you use to determine if these are sensitive to and representative of our multicultural society.

GOALS

1. To provide you the opportunity to analyze a textbook in terms of sensitivity to a multicultural society
2. To help you become more aware of the strengths and weaknesses in texts concerning multiculturalism

DIRECTIONS

A. Choose a textbook that is used in schools. If you are a teacher, choose a text you currently use in your class. If you are not a teacher, choose a book that you know is being used in schools or that was used as part of your own schooling.
B. Complete the Textbook Evaluation Form.

Discussion

1. Based on your analysis, what did you discover?
2. What are the best and worst features of this book in terms of sensitivity to cultures?
3. Would you recommend this book for use in school? Why or why not?
4. What patterns emerge when books are compared by educational levels (that is, elementary, middle, and high school)?
5. What patterns emerge when books are compared by content area?

Textbook Evaluation Form

Title:

Author:

Publisher/Date:

Grade/Use:

Does this book . . .	Yes	No	Somewhat
1. portray different cultural groups? Comments:			
2. avoid stereotypes in portraying cultural groups?			

Does this book . . .	Yes	No	Somewhat
Comments:			
3. present various groups in a manner that promotes respect for all people? Comments:			
4. avoid racist language? Comments:			
5. help children of all races and color feel proud of their background? Comments:			
6. help youngsters understand that there is diversity within each group of people? Comments:			
7. present objective information on the struggles of specific racial, cultural, and religious groups?			

Does this book . . .	Yes	No	Somewhat
Comments:			
8. promote democratic values that will help youngsters question prejudicial and stereotypic statements? Comments:			

Other comments based on your analysis of the book:

EXERCISE 52   CULTURAL ADVANTAGES AND DISADVANTAGES
_____

   Sometimes it is difficult to imagine advantages and disadvantages
based on culture. This exercise is designed to make it easier to
imagine them.

GOALS

1. To help you think about advantages and disadvantages you have
    because of race or cultural affiliation
2. To expose you to advantages and disadvantages that others have
    based on race and culture

DIRECTIONS

A. List advantages you believe you have in North American society
    based on your membership in your racial or cultural group. Also
    list disadvantages that you feel you have based on your member-
    ship.
B. Discuss your findings in small groups.

Discussion

1. Was it easier for you to list advantages or disadvantages?
2. Was there any pattern to either list? For example, did advan-
    tages tend to be in economics and education; did disadvantages
    tend to be in employment preference; and so on?
3. What did you learn about advantages and disadvantages based on
    other people's lists, as well as yours?

Version B

   This exercise can also be done by listing advantages and disadvantages of a racial or cultural group other than your own.

Racial or cultural group: _____

<u>Advantages</u>   <u>Disadvantages</u>

160

People usually have some accurate and inaccurate attitudes about racial and cultural groups. If any change is to occur in attitude, you need to examine your attitudes critically.

GOALS

1. To have you examine attitudes about racial and cultural groups
2. To help you initiate action to change certain attitudes

DIRECTIONS

A. Answer the following:
    1. Attitudes about other cultural groups that I presently hold:

    _____
    _____
    _____
    _____
    _____
    _____
    _____
    _____
    _____
    _____

    2. Put a plus (+) by those attitudes that you are satisfied with or do not wish to change.
    3. Put a minus (-) by those attitudes that you would like to change.
    4. What do you think you will need to help you change those attitudes you wish to change?
B. Choose someone in class who you think can help you change one (or more) of the attitudes that you labeled minus. Discuss this attitude with the person and tell him or her how and why he or she may be able to help you.
C. Together, make an agreement to work on changing this attitude. The agreement can be in the form of a written contract. This contract should specify the attitude(s) of focus, how your partner will help you change it, and specific times the two of you will meet to discuss progress toward your goal.

Attitudes about integration or separation of cultures are complex and, obviously, vary greatly. This exercise will help you compare and discuss your beliefs.

GOALS

1. To help you determine your stance on integration or segregation of races and cultures
2. To help you better understand the position of others on these issues

DIRECTIONS

A. This exercise can be done in small groups (8 to 10) or with the entire class, if it is small.
B. Put a long string on the floor and label one end "totally accept and hold view of racial and cultural integration." Label the other end "totally accept and hold view of racial and cultural separation."
C. Place yourself where you believe you belong on the continuum of the string.

Discussion

1. Discuss your position and those of others.
2. Those in the middle of the string discuss areas they think should be integrated and areas they think should be separated.
3. Those on the extremes discuss reasons for their position.

Most of us are more comfortable with some types of differences than we are with other types.

GOALS

1. To help you delineate your comfort with and acceptance of various groups
2. To help you explore your reasons for accepting some and not others

DIRECTIONS

A. Circle the number from the Comfort/Acceptance Scale that best describes your feelings and attitudes regarding each of the 30 items listed in the Accepting Others form.

Comfort/Acceptance Scale

1-very comfortable/accepting
2-fairly comfortable/accepting
3-neutral/no opinion
4-fairly uncomfortable/unaccepting
5-very uncomfortable/unaccepting

B. Discuss your completed forms in small groups.

Discussion

1. Which groups do you find acceptable and which not? What are your reasons for accepting or not accepting? Do you see patterns in your responses? In the responses of the small group?
2. What conclusions can you draw based on this exercise?
3. What have you learned about yourself from this exercise? _____

_____

_____

_____

_____

_____

Accepting Others

Group	I Am Comfortable/ Accepting			I Am Not Comfortable/ Not Accepting	
1. Neo-Nazi	1	2	3	4	5
2. Chicano	1	2	3	4	5
3. Afro-American	1	2	3	4	5
4. Wife abuser	1	2	3	4	5
5. Senile elderly person	1	2	3	4	5
6. Mentally retarded person	1	2	3	4	5
7. Catholic	1	2	3	4	5
8. Jew	1	2	3	4	5
9. Black Muslim	1	2	3	4	5
10. Italian	1	2	3	4	5
11. Prostitute	1	2	3	4	5
12. Homosexual	1	2	3	4	5
13. Drug pusher	1	2	3	4	5
14. Ex-convict	1	2	3	4	5
15. Ku Klux Klansman	1	2	3	4	5
16. Paraplegic	1	2	3	4	5
17. "Moonie"	1	2	3	4	5
18. Atheist	1	2	3	4	5
19. Iranian	1	2	3	4	5
20. Communist	1	2	3	4	5
21. Oriental-American	1	2	3	4	5
22. Overweight person	1	2	3	4	5
23. Genius	1	2	3	4	5
24. Alcoholic	1	2	3	4	5
25. Convicted rapist	1	2	3	4	5
26. Native American	1	2	3	4	5
27. Irish person	1	2	3	4	5
28. Millionaire	1	2	3	4	5
29. Cuban	1	2	3	4	5
30. Radical feminist	1	2	3	4	5

Almost every race or culture is subjected to debilitating stereotypes. This exercise encourages thinking about the effects of these stereotypes as well as the feelings of individuals who are subject to them.

GOALS

1. To recognize that various racial and cultural groups are subject to stereotypes
2. To attempt to understand the feelings of individuals subject to these stereotypes
3. To encourage you to examine the feelings you would have if you were subjected to stereotypes

DIRECTIONS

A. Fill out the Racial and Cultural Groups form. (Add others that are appropriate to your specific region.)
B. Think of one (or more) stereotype that you would resent were you a member of this race or culture.
C. Describe how you would react to this stereotype.
D. In small groups discuss your responses.

Discussion

1. What patterns emerged about the kinds of stereotypes people would resent?
2. What reactions and feelings did people have about being subjected to such stereotypes?
3. What insight do you have into the feelings of members of particular racial or cultural groups who are subject to these stereotypes?

Racial and Cultural Groups

Racial or Cultural Group	Stereotype(s) That I Would Resent If I Were a Member of This Group	My Reaction and Feelings about Being Subjected to This Stereotype(s)
1. Afro-American		
2. Puerto Rican		
3. Chicano		
4. Anglo-American		
5. Italian		
6. Irish		
7. Jewish		
8. Native American		
9. Amish		
10. Polish		
11. Chinese		
12. German		
Others:		

EXERCISE 57   THE JUST SOCIETY

This exercise will help you think about the kind of society that would be "just." You are encouraged to examine differences between a just society and the present reality.

GOALS

1. To have you think about racial and cultural justice
2. To help you prescribe changes that are needed in society

DIRECTIONS

A. Describe a society made up of rules and mores concerning race and culture that you see as fair and just. This imaginary society should be one that you would want to be born into without knowing what race or culture you would be.
B. In small groups discuss the different descriptions.

Discussion

1. What are the similarities and differences among group members?
2. What kind of society emerged? How similar or different is this ideal society from the current society?

As an addition to this exercise, given today's society as it is, what race or culture would you want to be? What race or culture would you not want to be? Discuss.

It is often difficult to understand the experience of a member of a race or culture other than your own. To be able to bridge some differences, it is important to grasp the reality of people different from yourself.

GOALS

1. To help you understand how it feels to be a member of another racial or cultural group
2. To help you see how present society affects the feelings and actions of members of other racial and cultural groups

DIRECTIONS

A. Relax and close your eyes. Imagine yourself as a member of another racial or cultural group.
B. You may want to imagine the following things from this perspective:
    1. How do you feel now?
    2. Where are you living?
    3. How do you feel about society?
    4. How do you feel about other cultures?
    5. What are some of your attitudes and behaviors?
C. Think about your attitudes toward the race or culture that you actually belong to.

Discussion

1. How would people be different if they belonged to a different race or culture?
2. What insights do you have about attitudes and actions of members of other races or cultures?

5

Recognizing and Dealing with Other Kinds of Prejudices and Stereotypes

INTRODUCTION

In Chapters 3 and 4 we included opportunities to examine prejudices and stereotypes related to sex and race. While such prejudices and stereotypes have been a central concern in North American society, they are by no means the only areas of bias. Prejudicial and stereo-typical attitudes and behaviors can have (and have had) deleterious effects on almost all areas of human experience. People experience prejudice and stereotyping because of age, physical disabilities, mental disabilities, giftedness, sexual preference, obesity, religious and political views--the list is considerable.

Bias regarding race and sex can so dominate the human relations curriculum that biases about other groups are either ignored or re-legated to the status of "less important." The point we want to emphasize is that prejudice and stereotyping, regardless of the focus or content, are based on similar characteristics:

limited and biased information
limited or no firsthand knowledge and experience with members of
  the group
unexamined attitudes

It would not be helpful to provide exercises on prejudice and stereotyping for a potpourri of "groups." First, the list would be impractically long (and probably incomplete); second, many of these issues might not be meaningful for all students. (Some issues are specific to particular regions.) Therefore, we have provided exercises about a few of these groups (the handicapped, the aged, the gifted, homosexuals) as examples. The rest of the exercises in this chapter (Exercises 70-78) are of a very general nature that can be readily applied to different issues. These general exercises were selected because they let you explore both your own attitudes and feelings and new information on the issues. For example, the fantasy exercise helps you think about what it would be like to be handicapped, obese, old, homosexual, and so on. It is through this kind of experience that an individual can begin to ask "How would I want to be treated by others? How would I react to typical prejudices and stereotypes aimed at me?"

We recommend that this chapter be used to explore issues that are mutually relevant to both students and instructors or that are unique to your own geographical area (for example, attitudes toward Amanans in Iowa and Amish in Pennsylvania). Students and instructors should construct the most meaningful curriculum possible.

It is hoped that by the end of this chapter both students and instructors will have clarified their attitudes about and knowledge of various kinds of people. It will be important for students to explore how certain prejudices and stereotypes may be different in nature. In addition, we hope that they will see the connections and patterns that underlie prejudicial and stereotypical thinking regardless of the specific issue. It is through such insight and understanding that thoughtful change can occur.

EXERCISE 59   EXPLORING ATTITUDES ABOUT HANDICAPPED PEOPLE

The U.S. Education for All Handicapped Children Act of 1975 (Public Law 94-142) gives all children, regardless of the type or degree of their handicap, the right to a free education. With it has come increased mainstreaming or the integrating of handicapped students into regular classrooms. Many of you may feel unprepared to deal with handicapped students and may find it difficult to overcome your own attitudes about them.

GOALS

1. To help you identify your own attitudes about handicapped people
2. To assist you in recognizing your strengths and weaknesses in working with handicapped students in a regular classroom
3. To give you an opportunity to discuss with others suggestions for dealing with specific types of handicaps

DIRECTIONS

A. List on the left below as many different handicaps as you can (for example, mental retardation, paralysis, blindness, hearing impairment).

Handicap   Reaction

_____   _____
_____   _____
_____   _____
_____   _____
_____   _____
_____   _____
_____   _____
_____   _____
_____   _____
_____   _____

B. When you come into contact with people with the above handicaps, what are your immediate reactions or feelings? Write them next to the handicap above.
C. Which handicaps do you think would be easiest to mainstream into a regular classroom? Which ones do you think would be most difficult to mainstream? Mark either an E (for easy) or a D (for difficult) by each of the handicaps.
D. In small groups, discuss items A through C above. Then discuss ways to prepare teachers and students for mainstreaming handicapped students into their classes.

It is hard to imagine what it must be like to live with a disability day after day with no hope of improvement or cure. Not knowing what it is like to be handicapped, teachers sometimes have trouble relating effectively to disabled people. For fear of offending or alienating, many of us choose what appears to be the easy way out--ignoring the handicapped or behaving as if we did not notice their handicaps. The purpose of this exercise is to help you confront the problem.

GOALS

1. To "experience" what it is like to be handicapped
2. To increase your empathy for the handicapped

DIRECTIONS

A. In pairs, take turns role-playing a handicapped person for an afternoon. For example, spend your time in a wheelchair or blindfolded as you endeavor to go about your regular daily activities. The partner acts as escort and observer, making notes.
B. Write down both negative and positive experiences you had while role-playing.

_____

_____

_____

_____

_____

C. In pairs or individually, interview a handicapped person. Inquire what responses or behaviors the handicapped person appreciates most and least from others.
D. Share your experiences with a small group that consists of three other pairs who also completed items A through C above.

Discussion

1. Based on your new knowledge and experience, list below your attitudes and behaviors you now consider to reflect empathy with handicapped people.

Empathic Attitudes	Empathic Behaviors

Gifted children are not necessarily always successful in school. This exercise is designed to help you think about why they sometimes fail.

GOALS

1. To explore your attitudes about giftedness
2. To help you think about how giftedness relates to success in school and in life

DIRECTIONS

A. Read the legend below and then decide which five characteristics in the chart (also below) are most important for each type of person listed. A characteristic may be used more than once. Use A, B, C, or D (as shown in the legend) to code the characteristics.

What five characteristics are most important
1. for a child to succeed in school (A)
2. for a child to be gifted (B)
3. for a child to be well-liked by teachers (C)
4. for an adult to be successful (D)

Mark A, B, C, or D	Characteristics
	Conforming
	Aggressive
	Creative
	Middle-class
	Artistic
	Manipulative
	Intelligent
	Curious
	Ambitious
	Witty
	Honest
	Handsome/beautiful
	Independent
	Competitive
	Hard working
	Obedient

Mark A, B, C, or D	Characteristics
	Popular
	Ethical
	Quiet
	Sensitive
	Respectful
	Charming
	Well-mannered
	Physically strong

B. In small groups discuss the ratings.

Discussion

1. What patterns emerged?
2. What implications do you see for gifted youngsters and their success in school or in adult life? Is success in school closely linked with being well-liked by a teacher?

Teachers, either deliberately or unknowingly, reward certain learning behaviors. These behaviors may vary depending on the type of student. It is important for you to realize that your rewards have an effect on your students.

GOALS

1. To help you explore the learning behaviors you reward as teachers
2. To help you examine your reward system for gifted students

DIRECTIONS

A. List the learning behaviors that you reward. For example, "I reward neat work," or "I reward extra effort."

_____

_____

_____

_____

_____

_____

_____

_____

_____

_____

B. Compare your lists in small groups. What patterns emerge?

Personal Notes

1. How do the behaviors you reward fit with what is known about learning behaviors in the gifted?
2. From your list, how successful do you think you would be with gifted students? Why?
3. If you wanted to make changes so that your reward system would be more appropriate to gifted students, what changes would you need to make? How could you make these changes?

It is important for you to examine your assumptions about how people learn and how learning may differ for different populations.

GOAL

To help you explore your views about how general youngsters, gifted youngsters, and adults learn.

DIRECTIONS

A.   List the main assumptions you have about how adults, general youngsters, and gifted youngsters learn. For example, you may assume that adults learn best when not graded or that general youngsters learn best when there is structure or that gifted youngsters learn best independently.
B.   Break into small groups and discuss similarities and differences about your assumptions.

Adults	General Youngsters	Gifted Youngsters

Discussion

1. How are the assumptions for general youngsters and gifted youngsters alike and how are they different?
2. In your experience are schools more likely to meet the learning needs of general youngsters or those of gifted youngsters?
3. Which group of youngsters is most like adults in learning behaviors? What implications does this have for you as a teacher?

Version B

This exercise can easily be adapted to other special populations. For example, instead of gifted youngsters, this exercise can be done with youngsters with learning disabilities or the mentally retarded.

Many of us have unexamined ideas about aging, some of which can be traced back to attitudes formed by the family.

GOALS

1. To have you recall early ideas about aging
2. To help you examine the validity of these ideas

DIRECTIONS

A. Complete each item as it applies to your family experience.
   1. When I was growing up, I heard the following comments about the elderly:_____

   _____

   _____

   _____

   _____

   _____

   2. In my family elderly were treated_____

   _____

   _____

   _____

   _____

   _____

   3. In my family elderly were believed to be_____

   _____

   _____

   _____

   _____

   _____

   4. In my family elderly women were_____

   _____

   _____

   _____

   _____

   _____

5. In my family elderly men were _____

    _____

    _____

    _____

    _____

    _____

B. In small groups discuss your responses.

Personal Notes

1. What trends emerged for you? _____

    _____

    _____

    _____

    _____

    _____

    _____

    _____

    _____

    _____

    _____

    _____

    _____

2. Of your responses to the items, which ideas do you think are still
    valid? Why? Which are not? Why? _____

    _____

    _____

    _____

    _____

    _____

    _____

    _____

    _____

    _____

    _____

As you grow older, important concerns in your life change. Some of these changes you may welcome; others you may fear. The realization that what is meaningful to you now may not be important later in life can help you keep concerns in perspective.

GOALS

1. To help you examine changes that happen with age
2. To help you think about concerns that may be associated with your older life

DIRECTIONS

A. From the following list of concerns enter in <u>Column A</u> those that were most significant in your childhood and early adolescence. In <u>Column B</u> list those that are most significant at your current age. In <u>Column C</u> list those that you think are significant for the elderly. For the purposes of this exercise a concern may not be listed more than once.

<u>Concerns</u>

Changes in health
Decreased income
Medical aspects
Sexual identity
Death and bereavement
Separation from employment
Increased free time
Family concerns
Loss of friends
Loss of spouse
Peer group
Fashions

Sexual activity
Responsibility for others
Mental quickness
Physical appearance
Proximity to death
Disability
Pastoral issues
Substance use and abuse
Sex-role perspectives
Financial concerns
Curfew
Achievement

B. Compare your columns. What changes do you notice? What pattern emerges for your elderly years?
C. After you have completed your columns, discuss them in small groups.

Column A	Column B	Column C

EXERCISE 66   ATTITUDES TOWARD OLD AGE

It is important for you to examine attitudes toward older people, because these attitudes may reflect what you assume about your own pending old age. Understanding your present attitudes may give insight into how you are preparing yourself for old age.

GOALS

1. To explore your attitudes about the elderly
2. To help you see your positive and negative attitudes about aging

DIRECTIONS

A. List ten adjectives that you associate with the elderly.

1.		6.	
2.		7.	
3.		8.	
4.		9.	
5.		10.	

B. Put a plus (+) next to those adjectives you view as positive descriptors, a minus (-) next to those that are negative, and a zero (0) next to those that are neutral.
C. What pattern has emerged for you? What does this say about your attitudes toward the elderly?
D. In small groups, discuss the patterns that emerged.

It is important for you to think about activities you enjoy and how these are or are not related to age. Some of these activities you can continue enjoying regardless of age, some perhaps you cannot. Enjoying activities, at any age, is important. This exercise gives you an opportunity to think about enjoying yourself at various ages.

GOALS

1. To help you clarify what activities you enjoy
2. To identify activities you may not be able to do when you are older
3. To help you find activities you can initiate in your elderly years

DIRECTIONS

A. List five activities that you enjoy doing.

1.

2.

3.

4.

5.

B. Of the five activities listed, which do you think you may not be able to do after the age of 65? Why?

Activities	Reasons

C. List five things that you think you will enjoy doing after the age of 65 but that you are not doing now.

1.

2.

3.

4.

5.

D. Why will you be able to do these things after age 65 but you cannot do now?_____

_____

_____

_____

_____

E. After completing these exercises, discuss your answers in small groups.

Discussion

1. What are the reasons given for discontinuing activities after age 65?
2. What are the reasons given for starting new activities after age 65 that cannot be done now?
3. What assumptions does the group make about activities and age? What evidence is given to validate these assumptions?

Emotion is sparked by the mention of certain topics. Homosexuality is one such topic. This exercise, designed to be completed alone or discussed in a group, attempts to help you focus on your feelings about homosexuality.

GOALS

1. To increase your awareness of your attitudes toward homosexuals
2. To help you differentiate among your levels (intensity) of feeling
3. To stimulate discussion among you about your attitudes

DIRECTIONS

A. Assign a value (1 through 5), using the Comfort Scale below, for each of the activities.

Comfort Scale

(1) Very uncomfortable
(2) Somewhat uncomfortable
(3) Neutral
(4) More or less comfortable
(5) Very comfortable

Activity	Comfort Level (number)
1. participating in a discussion about homosexuality	_____
2. reading about a gay-rights demonstration	_____
3. stopping to look at a vivid homosexual sketch in a restroom	_____
4. listening to a lecture by a gay person	_____
5. visiting a gay bar with friends	_____
6. being approached (solicited) by a homosexual	_____
7. having your child be taught by a gay fourth-grade teacher	_____
8. attending a gay party	_____
9. dancing with a homosexual who is your same sex	_____

B. Discuss the results of your "profile" with others.

[1]We recognize that homosexual men and lesbian women have distinctly different concerns. However, for the purpose of this workbook, we have used the terms *homosexual* and *gay* to refer to both homosexual men and lesbian women.

One issue of great controversy within education is whether homosexuals should be allowed to teach. This exercise stimulates consideration of this topic.

GOALS

1. To make you aware of differing attitudes toward gay teachers
2. To provide the opportunity for you to exchange points of view
    about gay teachers

DIRECTIONS

A. Draw a horizontal line on the board (at least 10 or 12 feet
    long), with each end "anchored" as depicted below:

    |_____|_____|

    Gays should not be   Ambivalent   OK for gays to
    allowed to teach   teach

B. Each of you make a mark on the continuum that best represents your
    opinion.
C. In small groups discuss the positions of your members.

Discussion

1. What general statement(s) can be made about the distribution on
    the continuum?
2. What are the arguments for allowing gays to teach?
3. What factors are there against gays being allowed to teach?
4. Do you feel differently toward an avowed gay teacher as compared
    to a teacher who is not gay? If so, explain these differences.

This exercise stimulates you to use your imagination. A set of questions guides you through the experience.

GOALS

1. To increase your awareness toward members of special populations
2. To increase your understanding of members of special populations

DIRECTIONS

A. Imagine that you are a member of a special population. Identify it.

_____
        (population)

B. Consider each of the following aspects of being a member of this group.
   1. How does it feel to be a member? _____

   _____

   _____

   _____

   _____

   _____

   2. How did you realize you were "different?" How did this aware-
      ness occur?_____

   _____

   _____

   _____

   _____

   _____

   3. What special problems, if any, do you have in school? (Use
      your own school as a reference.)_____

   _____

   _____

   _____

   _____

   _____

   4. What could teachers do to be helpful to you?_____

   _____

   _____

   _____

   _____

   _____

5. What other thoughts and feelings did you have as you imagined
    yourself being a member of this group?_____

    _____

    _____

    _____

    _____

    _____

    _____

    _____

    _____

    _____

    _____

    _____

C. In small groups discuss your reactions.

This exercise allows you to engage in some reading of your choice. In addition, you are to discuss your reactions to the reading.

GOALS

1. To stimulate learning about a special population
2. To exchange information about different populations

DIRECTIONS

A. Find a novel, medical bulletin or an article, or some other literature about a particular special population.
B. Read and react to the material.
C. Discuss the reading and your reactions with your small group.

Reactions

1. I noticed_____

_____

_____

_____

_____

_____

2. I didn't like_____

_____

_____

_____

_____

_____

3. I learned_____

_____

_____

_____

_____

_____

4. I wonder_____

_____

_____

_____

_____

_____

This exercise gives you the opportunity to gather some firsthand insight about thoughts and feelings of a member of a special population. If you are not a member of a special population, it may be difficult for you to understand certain realities they face. The more insight you have into the life experience of a member of a special population, the more likely it is that you will be able to communicate with such a person.

GOALS

1. To find out the thoughts and feelings of a member of a special population
2. To learn about issues facing him or her

DIRECTIONS

A. Conduct a personal interview with a member of a special population (for example, an elderly person, a gifted person, a Native-American, a homosexual, a handicapped person). Try to understand how this person thinks and feels.
B. Suggestions for interview questions:
   1. What is it like to be (Black, elderly, and so on) in this society?
   2. What special problems do you have because you are _____?
   3. What special advantages do you have because you are _____?
   4. What is the most important issue facing you as a member of this special group?
   5. What changes in society have been most helpful to you? Which are most needed?
   6. How can an educator best help members of your special group?
C. Discuss your reactions to the interview with your small group.

Discussion

1. What did you learn in your interview?
2. What were your feelings about the person you interviewed at the start and at the close of the interview?
3. From what you learned, what implications do you see for yourself as a person and as a potential teacher?
4. Has anything changed about your attitudes and feelings as the result of this interview? Share these changes with your group.

What if you suddenly had a different identity? How might your friends and family react to you if you were a member of a special population? This exercise leads you to explore these questions.

GOALS

1. To increase your self-awareness
2. To stimulate you to consider what belonging to a different population would be like
3. To encourage you to discuss how you are perceived by a friend or family member

DIRECTIONS

A. Assume a new identity. Have a different sex, age, race, or ability level. _____
                           (New Identity)
B. Think about how people who know you would react to you in your new identity. What would their reactions be?
    1. Family _____

    _____

    _____

    _____

    _____

    2. Friends _____

    _____

    _____

    _____

    _____

    3. Teachers _____

    _____

    _____

    _____

    4. Students _____

    _____

    _____

    _____

    _____

5. Employer _____

_____

_____

_____

_____

6. Other _____

_____

_____

_____

_____

C. As you review your responses to B, what insights do you have about these individuals and their attitudes? _____

_____

_____

_____

_____

_____

_____

_____

_____

_____

_____

D. Select a member from one of the above categories--for example, a family member. Explain the exercise and tell him or her the reactions you assumed he or she would have.
E. Explore with this person how accurate or inaccurate your assumptions were.
F. As a total group, discuss your own reflections about this exercise.

Stereotypes pervade society. Most people do not think about how these originated nor what purpose they serve. To stop perpetuating stereotypes, it is important for you to critically examine them.

GOALS

1. To recognize how stereotypes originate and how they are perpetuated
2. To recognize the function (purpose) of these stereotypes

DIRECTIONS

A. See the list of 20 stereotypes in the Stereotype Form.
B. In small groups determine and discuss the origin of the stereotype (this may take some extra research work), how it is perpetuated (television, certain novels, and so on), and its function (that is, what purpose is served by keeping this stereotype).

Discussion

1. What insights did the group have?
2. Did these stereotypes have more basis at one time in history than they do now?
3. What are the typical means of perpetuating these stereotypes?
4. Have there been any changes in the function of certain stereotypes over time?
5. Add and discuss other stereotypes if you wish.

Stereotype Form

Stereotype	Origin	How It Is Perpetuated	Function
1. Most Italians are connected to the Mafia			
2. Blondes are dumb			
3. Blacks are lazy			
4. Southern Whites are bigots			
5. Native Americans are drunks			
6. Jews are money-hungry			
7. Puerto Ricans are violent			
8. Feminists are sexually frustrated			
9. Women are emotional			
10. Chinese all look alike			
11. Gifted children are snobs			
12. Old people are senile			
13. The handicapped are retarded			
14. Germans are militaristic			
15. Homosexuals are promiscuous			
16. Irish are heavy drinkers			
17. Orientals are sly			
18. Catholics are papists			
19. Poles are stupid			
20. Men don't cry			

Humor has been studied and analyzed by scholars in many disciplines. This exercise allows you to examine your preferences and attitudes towards humor.

GOALS
1. To examine your individual sense of humor
2. To discover similarities within the group about what is and is not funny
3. To stimulate discussion about the role of humor in perpetuating stereotypes

DIRECTIONS

A. Each of you is to find a cartoon, comic strip, or joke (written) that features a stereotype or "putdown."
B. At the assigned time, share your examples.
C. Group the cartoons and jokes that none of you thinks are funny.
D. Compare the "funny" and "unfunny" cartoons or jokes. Consider these questions:
   1. Is "putdown" frequently used?
   2. Are the same stereotypes repeated?
   3. Why is one group of material considered humorous while the other is not?

Personal Notes

1. What feelings did you experience during the activity?

_____

_____

_____

Anger?_____ When?_____

_____

_____

Humor?_____ When?_____

_____

_____

Disgust?_____ When?_____

_____

_____

2. What did you learn during the activity?_____

_____

_____

_____

_____

3. To what extent do you believe cartoons *reflect* "putdowns,"
    and to what extent might they *cause* stereotypes?_____
    _____
    _____
    _____
    _____

You have had an opportunity to share several experiences and exercises with the same people. Each of the members has been able to observe others. Capitalize on these observations by sharing. *Note to instructors:* This can be given as a homework assignment.

GOALS

1. To receive feedback about behavior
2. To stimulate self-awareness
3. To provide opportunity for personal goal setting

DIRECTIONS

A. Write items of feedback on separate sheets of paper for each member of the group. Fold each sheet and write the name on the outside. Some examples: "I like the way you add to the group's information." "I don't like it when you interrupt me." "Your smile is infectious and helps the group." "You often say you're not sexist, but you often describe men and women in very stereo-typed ways." Short behavioral descriptions can be more useful to the receiver than long paragraphs.
B. Collect the sheets with your name on them. Read them over. Gather the descriptions that are given more than once.

Personal Notes

1. How the group sees me: _____

_____

_____

_____

_____

_____

_____

_____

2. What pleases me about the way the group sees me:_____

_____

_____

_____

_____

_____

_____

_____

3. What I'd like to change about myself based on the comments in the group:_____

_____

_____

_____

_____

_____

_____

_____

The purpose of this exercise is to give group members a chance to set a goal within the group.

GOALS

1. To follow up on the group-feedback activity (Exercise 76)
2. To stimulate personal change among group members
3. To allow the group to experience helping individual members

DIRECTIONS

A. Share your responses to the last item in Exercise 76 ("What I'd like to change about myself in the group").
B. You can help each other the most not by giving advice but by helping members clarify what they wish to change.
C. Each of you selects *one* behavior to work on. This behavior should be something that can be observed and evaluated by the group.
D. After each of you has shared the behavior you wish to change, you should enter into a written contract with the group, using the Contract Form.

Contract Form

Name: _____

Date of contract: _____

The behavior I wish to change: _____

_____

_____

_____

Group Role: (The procedures that group members will employ to help
you make the desired change. The procedures should include how
members will observe the behavior, give feedback, and evaluate change.)

_____

_____

_____

_____

_____

_____

_____

_____

_____

Date of Contract Completion:_____

Group members may wish to discuss what they have learned about themselves, their attitudes, and their values.

GOALS

1. To provide an activity to close the course
2. To stimulate individual recall of earlier activities
3. To stimulate sharing among group members

DIRECTIONS

A. Form a round table setting with all of you in full view of each other.
B. Express personal feelings, specific interests, and high points of the group's activities.
C. Take turns completing these items regarding your group experience:
    1. I remember when we . . .
    2. I learned the most when . . .
    3. I found out that I . . .
    4. The most fun for me was when . . .
    5. What I think will have the most lasting impact is . . .
    6. What I learned that will help me be a more effective teacher is . . .
    7. Other . . .

A

Appendix: Glossary

Age discrimination Treating people in a negative manner because of their age.

Ageism Attitudes and actions directed toward older people based on the belief that aging makes one undesirable and less useful to society.

Careful attending Listening for more than the words of a message, while indicating interest.

Communication skills Learned competencies that improve the quality of interaction among people.

Confrontation Using communication skills in a situation that focuses on a personal issue of meaning to the participants.

Cultural pluralism A system of society in which various subgroups (usually ethnic) have equal power in the decision-making process. Various cultures can maintain their identity and still participate in the mainstream of society.

Ethnic group A group that has a common social and cultural heritage. Usually has a distinctive pattern of family life, religion, and language.

Ethnic studies Academic field dealing with the uniqueness and richness of specific racial or cultural groups, including their historical and cultural knowledge.

Ethnocentrism The tendency to view one's ethnic group or culture as superior to others.

Feedback Description of a person's behaviors and, at times, personal reaction to those behaviors.

Genuineness A form of self-disclosure that includes the speaker's specific feelings.

Giftedness According to the U. S. Office of Education's definition, gifted students show potential or consistently excel in one or more of the following areas--general intellectual ability, specific academic aptitude, creative thinking, leadership ability, and skill in the visual and performing arts--to the extent that they can benefit from specifically planned educational services.

Handicap A disadvantage that makes achievement unusually difficult. A handicapped person usually requires special resources in order to have an equal opportunity to succeed.

Human interaction The interchange between two or more people in terms of their commonality (humanness) and their individuality.

Human relations training Instruction that recognizes the humanness of people. All people have a common bond by the mere fact that they are human.

Mainstreaming The moving of handicapped children from segregated special classes to regular classes.

Minority group A group that can be distinguished by a feature such as race, culture, sex, or age, and is numerically smaller than the majority in a particular situation.

   Special Note: It is common usage to consider minority groups as those that have not received equal access to opportunities in society. According to this definition women would be considered a minority group. However, we consider *minority group* in its strict meaning of "less than the majority." In our definition, women are not a minority group. However, because of sexism, women as a group have not gotten equal access or treatment in North American society. Thus, we differentiate the numerical minority from the victims of oppression.

Multicultural education Integration of human relations training and ethnic studies.

Nonsexist education Education that fosters the development of the full range of skills, knowledge, and interests of both males and females.

Open questions Those that require more than a yes or no response.

Paraphrase A shortened version of a message that changes some of its words but retains its meaning.

Prejudice Connotes prejudgment. Dislike of or hostility to individuals or groups based on preconceived notions.

Racism Attitudes and practices based on the belief that certain races are inherently superior to others.

Reflecting feelings Repeating a message in a manner that highlights the feelings in it.

Restatement A word-for-word repetition of the content of a message.

Self-disclosure A message in which the speaker gives an opinion, value, past experience, or the like.

Sexism Attitudes and practices based on the belief that one sex is superior to the other and that certain roles and functions in a society are inherently determined by sex.

Stereotyping Oversimplified generalization about a particular group or individuals within it. Usually carries derogatory implications.